THE ORIGINAL ARTICLE

This gardening text, first published over fifty years ago, seems more pertinent today than ever. Written by two pioneers in Bio-Dynamic agriculture, Ehrenfried Pfeiffer and Erika Riese, it contains many hard-earned truths gained from years of loving, hands-on experience and deep insights. Such wisdom is hard to come by anywhere, and unusual to find in print.

Their concern for the environment and for providing a more healthful nutrition is clear, but so is their wish to create a truly productive garden. They were writing this book as the term "Victory Garden" was evolving in the World War II era. Small, productive gardens would provide extra food for each household and conserve resources for the war effort. But in combining concerns for productivity, healthful nutrition and the environment, they created what is today the ideal manual for the modern gardener, be it for the small or even market grower.

Some things in the book may seem outdated like the name of specific seed varieties or even the name of a chapter like "Manifesto to the Housewife." But, with equal respect to the reader and the writers, we have, in this re-printing made no changes -- used no additives -- preserving the full flavor of the original text.

Mac Mead
Chestnut Ridge, NY

GROW A GARDEN
AND BE SELF-SUFFICIENT

EHRENFRIED PFEIFFER *and* ERIKA RIESE

GROW A GARDEN
AND BE SELF-SUFFICIENT

MERCURY PRESS

This MERCURY PRESS edition, first published in 1981,
is an unabridged and unaltered republication of the book first published
by the Anthroposophic Press in 1942.

ISBN: 978-1-957569-53-6

Table of Contents

Index

Preface

THE INTENTION of this book is to present some practical
guide lines and experiences for the homestead gardener and
the home gardener. It is written to meet the practical needs of the
amateur as well as of those who must support themselves and
therefore dispenses with all theoretical frills. Particular care has
been devoted to the chapter on fertilizing because this field is usually neglected in garden practice. Moreover, the soil-conserving
and fertility-maintaining humus processes have been given promi-
nence in preference to procedures which give highest yields at
the cost of the soil's lasting health. During the last sixteen years
the authors have applied the Bio-Dynamic Method with success
and feel obliged to include some statements about it. They are
supported in this by the results obtained in regard to soil improvement and the quality of the vegetables grown by this
method. Those who have no interest in the Bio-Dynamic Method
or feel called upon to reject it can, nevertheless, use these practical
instructions in their gardens. The authors have tried to present
the material in a way that will leave everyone free to do as he
thinks best. They are confident that the gardens, when cultivated
in the manner indicated in this book, will speak for themselves.
In the gardening and agricultural literature of today there are,
perhaps, ten books available dealing exclusively with mineral fertilizing to one which treats of humus-forming organic methods.
It cannot, therefore, be termed prejudice to place the latter in
the foreground, but, on the contrary, it is the "restoration of a
necessary balance."

In any case, the authors of the book are ready to assist the reader and offer advice for the planning of his garden, or to clarify and amplify the instructions necessary to meet special conditions.

We must still express our thanks and appreciation to the countless friends who have assisted in the preparation of this book.

Kimberton Farms,   E. PFEIFFER and E. RIESE
Phoenixville, Penna.,
September 1941

1. Successful Gardening for the Small Landholder

SELF-SUFFICIENCY is a necessity which arises out of the problems of the present economic system, and which will contribute to the solution of these problems. It is a necessity for the farmer who wishes to preserve the fertility of the land eventually to be inherited by his children. Not only must the farmer be worthy of what has been entrusted to him, but he must build his means of production on a solid foundation. When he has accomplished this first task, he can begin to think of cash crops which will provide him the money to buy the things he cannot himself produce.

But the idea of self-sufficiency extends beyond the farmer; it reaches the small landholder who is compelled, through force of circumstances, to wring a living out of a small acreage. It offers an opportunity as well to the man with a modest income from another source who owns a small piece of land and wishes to keep in touch with the productive forces of nature. It provides even for the city dweller, tired of stone walls and paved streets, the joy of having a little piece of the earth's surface on which to cultivate flowers and vegetables in his leisure hours, if for no other reason than to discover that there is nothing so enjoyable and healthful as tasty, homegrown vegetables, ripened on his own fertile soil, moistened by the rains, swept by the winds and shone upon by the sun, cultivated and raised through his own efforts, cooked and eaten the very day they are picked.

Those who thus come into contact with nature's living forces soon find that no food chemistry, no adding to or subtracting from the food they eat can improve on nature's original product. Such people, whatever their motives for acquiring small garden plots, be it duty, pleasure, business, recreation, or the finding of a balance for mechanical or intellectual pursuits, all such people wish to succeed in their venture. But to succeed means a co-ordination of careful planning and skillful execution.

The ethical, as distinguished from the economic values, should also be appreciated. We can understand this when we observe the phenomena of growth, when we become conscious of the changing seasons as shown in the fluctuations of the weather, in the warmth and light of the sun; we experience this in the pleasure we have in watching the gradual development of plant life, in the quickening of the movement of the blood in our veins as we till the soil, as we weed the rank growths and harvest the good and useful. All these things have values not measurable in dollars and cents. Indeed, their ultimate value lies in their power to build character. A man who loves the soil develops a finer awareness of the synthesizing processes and a sense for the upbuilding forces in the world; and he cares less and less for the more destructive processes of analysis. Gradually he becomes the bearer of a new mentality, capable of perceiving the permanent truths of life itself. The physical basis, however, for the small, but successful holding has to be built first. This is the primary task.

From a practical point of view, the small garden should furnish food, if not all, at least abundant food. And we must never forget that the beautiful flowers that grow in our garden are food in another sense—food for eyes and nose. The most commercialized garden can create a balance of beauty, while, at the same time, fulfilling certain biological health requirements, making a total biological unit.

The smallholder's garden, if planted and tended in accordance with the laws of nature, of life and maintenance, is a living being—a biologically sound totality—whether with respect to the principle of self-sufficiency, healthy growth, or human food

2

requirements. Monoculture is out of the question in such a unit. Neither the soil nor our stomachs would stand it. The balanced diet necessary for the maintenance of health presupposes a balanced production.

Proper planning requires first of all an orientation with regard to our needs. The human being annually eats six, seven or eight times his own weight. The annual food consumption per head in the United States, according to statistics, is as follows:

Carbohydrates:	Bread and other flour products	230	pounds
	Potatoes	180	"
	Sugar	100	"
Proteins etc.:	Milk	200	"
	Meat (including fish and fowl)	166	"
	Eggs	36	"
	Nuts etc.	20	"
Living energy:	Vegetables	300	"
	Fruit (including citrus fruits and tomatoes)	72	"
	Oils and fats (including butter)	44	"
		1348	pounds

This, however, allows a wide margin for the individual. In support of this we quote from Gove Hambidge's interesting study *Your Meals and Your Money.** Table A represents the minimum diet requirements for people who try to save money on food and who are indifferent to the progress in dietetic knowledge. Table B represents the best diet in terms of calories, starches, proteins, minerals, vitamins, etc.

PLAN A.

Mr. Hambidge comments on Table A as follows: "This . . . is a restricted diet for emergency use. There can be little question but that large numbers of people in America habitually live on a diet that is less nearly adequate and less intelligently devised.

* Whittlesey House. McGraw-Hill Book Co.

PLAN A—Yearly

Group	Child Under 4	Boy 4-6 Girl 4-7	Boy 7-8 Girl 8-10	Boy 9-10 Girl 11-13	Boy 11-12 Girl Over 13 Moderately Active Woman	Active Boy 13-15 Very Active Woman	Active Boy Over 15	Moderately Active Man	Very Active Man
1. Flour, cereals, pounds	85	140	175	195	195	280	370	280	455
or Bread, pounds	40	65	80	90	90	130	170	130	210
Flour, cereals, pounds	60	95	120	135	135	195	255	195	315
2. Milk, quarts	182	182	182	182	182-365	182-365	182	91	91
3. Potatoes, sweet potatoes, pounds	100	110	125	140	140	160	225	160	300
4. Dried beans, peas, nuts, pounds	—	8	18	20	25	30	30	40	50
5. Tomatoes, citrus fruits, pounds	50	50	50	50	50	50	50	50	50
6. L. g. y. vegetables, pounds	30	30	45	50	50	40	25	40	25
7. Dried fruits, pounds	3	3	6	8	10	15	10	15	10
8. Other vegetables, fruits, pounds	12	20	30	40	45	50	50	50	50
9. Fats, pounds	10	20	30	30	35	55	65	55	75
10. Sugars, pounds	8	20	30	40	45	65	70	70	80
11. Lean meat, poultry, fish, pounds	—	5	15	22	28	35	35	40	50
12. Eggs, dozens	10	10	10	8½	8½	7½	6	6	6

4

PLAN B—Yearly

Group	Child Under 4	Boy 4-6 / Girl 4-7	Boy 7-8 / Girl 8-10	Boy 9-10 / Girl 11-13	Boy 11-12 / Girl Over 13 / Moderately Active Woman	Active Boy 13-15 / Very Active Woman	Active Boy Over 15	Moderately Active Man	Very Active Man
1. Flour, cereals, pounds	45	55	65	65	65	105	125	125	200
or Bread, pounds	30	45	60	60	60	120	150	150	240
Flour, cereals, pounds	25	25	25	25	25	25	25	25	40
2. Milk, quarts	365	365	365	365	365	365	240-365	182	182
3. Potatoes, sweet potatoes, pounds	100	100	100	100	110	150	300	150	350
4. Dried beans, peas, nuts, pounds	—	2	3	5	5	10	10	10	10
5. Tomatoes, citrus fruits, pounds	75	75	80	90	110	120	120	120	120
6. L. g. y. vegetables, pounds	60	75	90	90	120	150	180	180	180
7. Dried fruits, pounds	5	5	8	10	15	25	30	25	30
8. Other vegetables, fruits, pounds	140	200	300	300	300	350	400	400	400
9. Fats, pounds	10	15	27	35	40	65	80	65	100
10. Sugars, pounds	7	15	30	35	40	75	115	75	115
11. Lean meat, poultry, fish pounds	10	40	90	120	150	200	250	220	250
12. Eggs, dozens	25	30	30	30	30	30	30	30	30

But the point is, don't use it unless you have to. Get away from it as soon as you can."

The proportion given provides a kind of starvation diet, but is often used by those ignorant of the problems of nutrition.

The opposite extreme is the diet in Table B which gives the very best proportions.

PLAN B.

Mr. Hambidge in giving this example says: "This is a liberal diet. Aim to get as near it as possible. It will pay in terms of well-being even if you have to economize on some other expenses."

A comparison of the two tables reveals the increasing demand for vegetables and fruit, and that is the very thing the small-holder's garden can contribute: greater health values. It is another proof that *what is biologically right is economically sound* and healthful too.

The planting system herein described, and worked out in practice through many years, enables the smallest and poorest holder, as well as the great landowner, to produce with the least effort that which the body requires.

Moreover, whoever likes to dig deeper in the truths of nature will be surprised and pleased to discover how justly the good earth works to build up a closed biological unit—the little garden—in order to support that other closed biological unit—man himself.

2. Basic Considerations for the Home Garden

WE MUST TAKE three different aspects into consideration when planning the home garden; our needs, the size of the garden, and the quality of the soil. The primary, basic aspect is the soil quality. We also include, in this classification, the environmental conditions, especially climate. The intensity of cultivation is dependent upon it. In a rain-poor climate a dry, sandy soil forms little humus, is quickly warmed by the sun; but cools off quickly, too. On cool, clear nights it is liable to frosts and hoar frosts; on hot days the sand becomes overheated through reflection. A permanent ground cover and shading of the soil is necessary here. The cultures must be selected and mixed so that this is possible at all times. Such soils can be planted very early in the Spring, as soon as it begins to get warm. We must remember, however, that they are very susceptible to night frosts. If a great deal of humus is added to them they are not unfit for early seed beds and portable cold frames.

A wet, tough, clay-soil stands at the opposite pole. It is cold, warms slowly, drys slowly; in wet weather it can be worked with difficulty or not at all. Lack of proper soil drainage is its worst enemy. With such a soil everything depends upon the correct moment of cultivation. The gardener must wait until it is dry enough and then work quickly. The ability to handle a heavy soil correctly is achieved only through long experience. Particular care should be taken that a heavy soil can freeze through well in winter, that is, it should be left rough ploughed or rough spaded. The beds, especially in or after wet periods, should also be heaped up and rounded so that more air penetrates and the water can run

7

off and evaporate. Deep-rooting legumes should be used, for their remedial effect, in the cultivation of heavy soils.

The ideal soil is the humus type, having a loose and crumbly structure, and a rich content of ripe, earthy, organic matter. It responds quickly to cultivation; the soil life of bacteria and earthworms cares for its permanent renewal. Its excellence is so great that every measure for the maintenance and furtherance of the humus structure is justified, even if this means labor and expense. The friable, healthy condition, once attained, spares labor and strength and fully repays our original investment of time and energy. Proper treatment makes us independent of the soil type, whether, for example, it is sandy or clayey. A humus-bound sand, with some clay content, is, with the right care and continued compost and manure fertilizing, just as fertile as a humus-filled clay soil. The extremes are brought into balance by the humus content and the humus condition.

The lay of the land is also important. Level stretches should be elevated in order to regulate the air and water content. Wind protection must be provided for in the layout. (Wind-breaks.) Steep slopes should be terraced in order to gain land, to facilitate cultivation and to avoid gullying and sheet erosion. The garden beds should be laid out at right angles to the slope and in contour, otherwise the upper areas will become poorer and poorer, and good soil will be washed down to the foot. The intense radiation of the sun on a southern slope must be compensated for with shade. On a northern slope it may be necessary to provide for a thinner stand. In rolling or hilly land the planting should follow the line of the ridges.

The size of the home garden is usually a given one. This plus the quality of the soil determines the approximate, possible yield. However, the experienced gardener, with soil-conserving crop rotations, maintenance of humus content, correct soil cultivation, and the selection of suitable varieties, can, perhaps, harvest double as much from the same soil as the novice. Thus, the yield

8

still depends upon the person and his labor. Nevertheless, there are certain figures, derived from experience, on the basis of which it is possible to foresee how nearly a given size and productivity will meet the given needs.

The basis for calculating the total food needs of one human being, in the temperate zone, is an area of about one and one-quarter acres (6000 sq. yds.) in a medium heavy soil with humus content. That, however, is still not the total area necessary for complete self-support. Self-sufficiency requires the maintenance of the means of production, that is, the land should be kept in a permanently vital state, with the fertilizer produced on the place itself. A small amount of livestock is therefore included under the heading of self-sufficiency, in order to maintain the land. The provision of their feed requires a small ploughed field and some meadow and hayland, in addition to the garden area. The plans of the holding are then made so as to allow for the production of some cash crops, such as milk, fruit, honey, vegetables, potatoes, pigs, eggs, etc., in order to meet other living costs—clothing, repairs on the house and tools, school, doctor, taxes, and occasional recreation.

Let us, therefore, make the following classification derived from a consideration of the needs of one family or another: A. partial self-support, especially in regard to vegetables, which is possible with the home garden; B. complete self-sufficiency with respect to food, which is, perhaps, possible on a middle sized homestead with some help from outside (meat, fertilizer); C. the smallest sized farm which makes possible a completely independent subsistence—meets the needs of a modest, but independent existence.

A. PARTIAL SELF-SUFFICIENCY, CHIEFLY IN RESPECT TO VEGETABLES

In the temperate zone, in a medium heavy soil, a home garden of about 1000 square feet can, with good care, yield an approximate total of from 625 to 700 lbs. of a variety of vegetables. In the

9

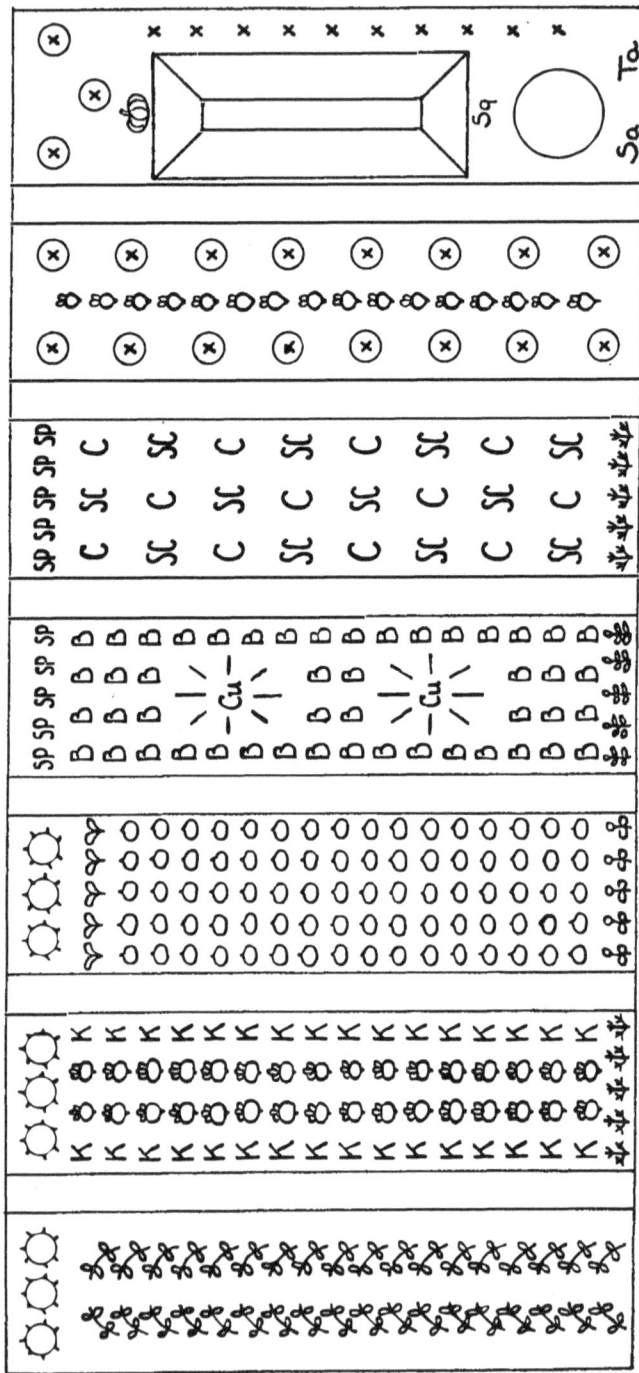

Planting Plan for a 30 ft. by 30 ft. Garden.

T Tomatoes   SC Early Savoy Cabbage   O Onion   Peas   B Bush Beans

Sq Squash   C Cabbage, Broccoli   K Kohl-rabi   DP Dwarf Peas   C Cucumber

Pumpkin   RC Red Cabbage, Sprouts   S Swiss Chard, Spinach   SP Sugar-Podded Peas   L Lettuce

Sq   Sa   Ta

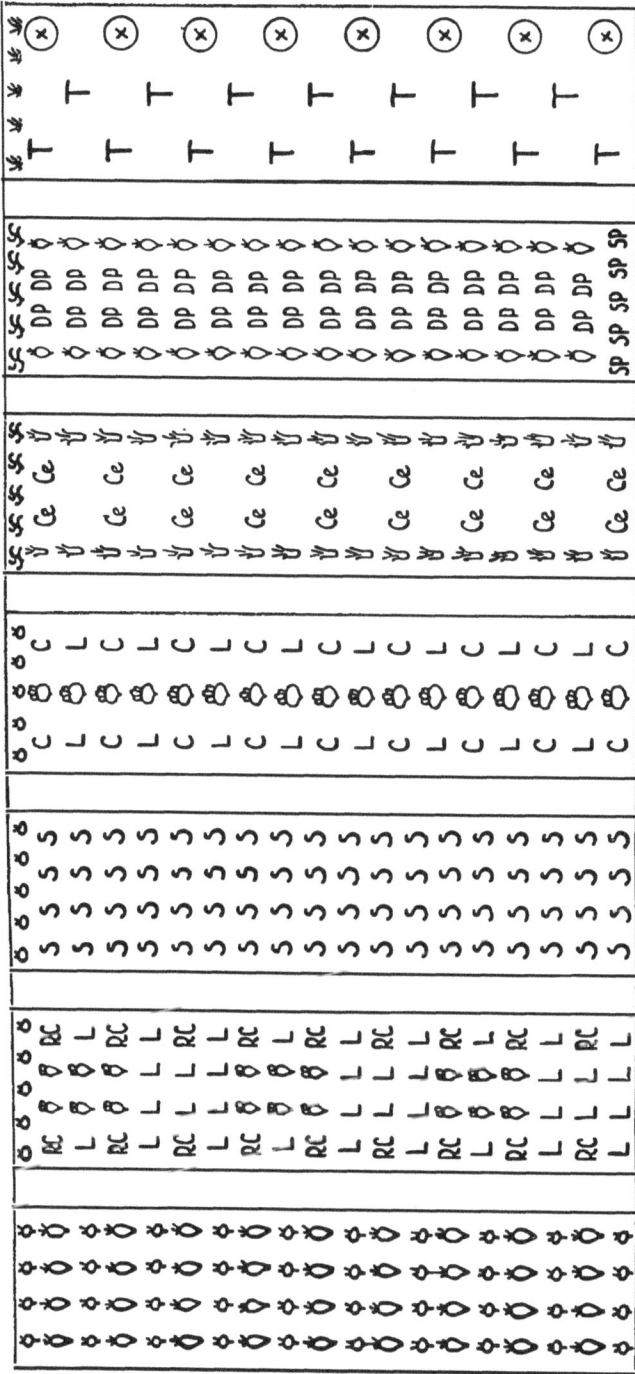

3'6"

10"

ᦔ Beet	ᛉ Carrots, Turnips
ଃ Summer Radish	୪ Shallots, Garlic
ᕬ Early Radish	ᨆ Leek
ᚨ Red Radish	Ce Celery

⊗ Pole Beans	‡ Summer Savory
× Corn	✿ Dill
☼ Sunflower	

⊶ Borage	⚘ Sweet Marjoram
ᨒ Chives	Ta Tarragon
ℱ Parsley	Sa Sage

case of a mixed, soil-conserving planting, these are distributed as follows:

Average Yield of a Home Garden of 30 by 36 feet (14 beds).

Width of beds 4 feet, length 15 feet.

	No. Plants	Pounds	Pieces
Pole Beans	27	176	
Sweet Corn	9	9	20
Tomatoes	15	66	
Kohl-rabi	50	11	
Cabbage	29	88	
Early Savoy Cabbage	14	26	
Bush Beans	50	22-26	
Peas	4 rows	22	
Cucumbers	2	11	
Onions	85	31-35	
Beets	3 rows	26	50
Carrots[1]	6 rows	20	
Sugar Peas	18	11-13	
Leeks	32	9-13	
Celeriac[2]	18	13	
Red Cabbage	18	44-50	
Lettuce[3]	46	31	46
Swiss Chard	4 rows	13-23	
Shallots		9-11	
Winter Squash	1	23-35	
Zucchini Squash	1	11-18	
Herbs			

672-723 lbs.

[1] Frequently 2-3 beds of carrots are sown.
[2] A full bed of celeriac yields 26 lbs.
[3] With skillful interplanting it is possible to grow 100-200 heads of lettuce in the above garden plan.

This list is not, of course, a final or complete one. It can easily be changed according to individual taste and climatic conditions. One gardener may prefer to plant more corn and less kohl-rabi. Another may wish to have lima beans and eggplant and some peppers, or melons and pumpkins and celery. There may even be people who are very fond of parsnips!

A study of such a table leads us to the significant conclusion that there is a definite relationship between man and the biological laws of nature. For the mixed cultures and rotation of crops which alone guarantee the maintenance of soil fertility parallel the variety evident in the nutritive needs of the human being. A monoculture of potatoes, red cabbage, beans, or onions is a biological absurdity. And a man who tries to live solely on potatoes, or red cabbage, or beans, or onions, will certainly become aware that this, too, is fully as absurd. Both the soil and the human being require a variety of vegetables, frequent change and, from time to time, a spice, a bit of green or an herb. Even the most modest home garden is thus an image of the whole man with respect to his needs and his demands.

The finest social ideas do not help much if a man is hungry or suffers deficiencies due to a restricted diet. The greatest philanthropist and social reformer must first plunge down into the material concerns of those under his care. His first task is to provide instruction and make possible the satisfaction of their daily requirements.

In general the vegetable supply of 3-4 persons can be produced in a home garden such as the one described at the beginning of this discussion. Both the philanthropist and the beginner, however, may think it difficult to produce 625-700 pounds of vegetables on such a small piece of land. Nevertheless, the increasing efficiency of the gardener and the manageable size of the garden contribute toward making this possible. Hundreds of gardeners under the supervision of the writer have already obtained such yields.

B. COMPLETE SELF-SUFFICIENCY WITH RESPECT TO FOOD

According to the tables quoted in Chapter I, the vegetable needs of a family of 2 adults and 3 children amount to between 660 and 1450 pounds. The area necessary for the production of this total lies between 1000 and 3000 square feet, depending upon individual needs, the type of soil and climate. On a small homestead, from 10,000 to 55,000 square feet in area, it is possible to approach or even reach a basis of support which includes the chief elements of nutrition. As an example of the smaller size we will consider one of 13,500 square feet which we observed in all its stages.

The owner, who is an industrial worker, put his first savings into the purchase of this piece of land. Then with the help of a small loan he built his house.

He divided the land into three sections: 4500 square feet were used for the vegetable garden, 4500 were occupied by the house and a small lawn and flower garden, the remaining 4500 were seeded down to meadowland.

In his vegetable garden he followed all the principles of the bio-dynamic method; compost and manure treatment, crop rotation, mixed cultures, etc. Moreover, he kept some poultry, attended to such matters as fencing, laying paths and building a road. All these activities were carried on in his spare time, outside working hours.

After three years the stand of vegetables in his garden was excellent and more than enough to fill the requirements of his household. In fact, with the cash obtained from selling the surplus yield, he was able to cover additional household costs (bread, meat, milk), as well as one third of his taxes.

Many other factory workers living near him have successfully followed in his footsteps. A carefully devised crop rotation along the lines described in this book enables such homesteaders to do all the work on their land in spare time with a minimum of effort.

C. INDEPENDENCE ON FIVE TO SEVEN ACRES.

(Subsistence Minimum)

The original prototype of healthy self-sufficiency is the small farmer's holding of a size which just maintains a family. This size is conditioned by climate, soil type, amount of moisture and water supply. Such a holding furnishes a standard for the entire locality which has to reckon with the same conditions. On a small farm, with a good ratio between tilled fields, pasture, and hayland, its manure production can be brought into balance with its crop requirements. Under a crop rotation of not less than 4-6 years, diversified planting supplies food (bread, potatoes) for the household, fodder and straw (litter) for the cattle, as well as milk and meat. We assume that the farmer and his wife do not deny themselves chickens (eggs), and a small vegetable and herb garden. In highly cultivated agricultural regions, we find flower gardens, as well, and always, of course, fruit trees and bees.

It has been demonstrated over a period of more than sixteen years, that such biologically sound farm units maintain the fertility of the soil without any loss of nutritive substances. A small farm with 40 to 60% tilled land, and a corresponding amount of pasture and hayland for the support of a proportionate number of cattle, can maintain itself and in addition produce cash crops on one to two fifths of the cultivated area. This is accomplished by means of a long-term crop rotation, with not more than two grain years and at least one legume year in a five-year period. A holding of this type can thus provide money for needs other than food (such as taxes, medicine, clothing and education).

An area which suffices for the maintenance of a cow, a calf and a steer gives us the smallest unit. Add to this the area devoted to food for the human beings, at least one and a quarter acres per person, a certain "fertility reserve," and the area assigned to cash crops. It follows, that a small holding of from five to seven and a half acres represents the smallest healthy unit on soil of average quality, in a region with medium rainfall (30-35 inches). The acreage is divided thus: one fifth for vegetables, three fifths for pasture and hayland, one fifth for grain and fodder.

A detailed division of the garden area will grow out of the particular needs, whether for instance we wish to have all kinds of vegetables, or do not need to be self-sufficient and can use our piece of land for flowers, berry bushes, and dwarf or espalier fruit trees. We repeat that a one-sided culture of potatoes, cabbage, turnips, or onions, is unhealthy for the soil. In the sense of a well-regulated crop rotation, such a one-sided culture must be compensated for in the next year. Moreover, such a "provider" would certainly have a monotonous diet, and would soon be obliged to seek a balance.

The essential place for fruit trees, berries, grapes and flowers, in the garden, is still to be discussed. Although monocultures are out of the question, these plants can play a useful as well as an ornamental role in the protective and boundary plantings of a larger plan. A low berry hedge can be used to fence off an area from a neighboring piece of land or from the street, or to line a path. Ordinarily, trees shade a garden too much, but when planted so as to shade a path, the liquid manure barrel, the compost yard, or even a summer house they are in their proper place. We recommend the creation of an enclosed space for every individual garden or small group of gardens. This recommendation is based on biological fundamentals, such as shade, ripeness of the soil, protection of the soil's carbonic acid content, and to break the force of the wind. A permanent or perennial hedge can be made of bushes or grapevines and an annual hedge of sunflowers, sweet corn, or pole beans. Flowers and medicinal and kitchen herbs are suitable for bordering beds and paths. Thus it is possible to create an enclosed growing space with comparatively simple means.

Community Planning of Gardens and Homesteads.

In recent years small gardens have sprung up everywhere on the outskirts of cities and industrial districts and in suburban areas. Their growth is often arbitrary and rather inorganic. This is especially true when the owners of adjoining gardens plan, each for himself, without regard for the larger pattern. The disturbed picture which results illustrates the urgent need for large scale planning in such areas. These plans should be made beforehand and used educationally in order that sound and organic units may be built up.

However, this sort of predetermined shaping of the landscape is still sadly neglected in the world today. Even cities which provide important park areas in their central portions straggle out inorganically, dismembered, raglike into their environs. The suburban areas stretch out into dead-end streets lined with wretched little buildings. Beyond these we enter a sort of wasteland half-wild, weedy and strewn with dump heaps. The city land prices, which depend upon industrial, street and railroad developments and on the growing sea of houses, have long since condemned such areas to sterility. The farmers have moved away. Because of the nearness to market, truck gardens with hot houses have sprung up here and there. In general, this outlying area lies idle. Scarcely anything is changed in the landscape of the city's environment when such a zone is placed at the disposal of the poor for gardens. These tiny gardens, with self-constructed cottages or just packing box sheds, separated from one another with wire or wooden fences, may be a source of satisfaction for the individual. Here and there are a few flowers or some vegetables. Perhaps some especially ingenious person has made a rock or herb garden, or even a pool with water plants, where he can sit of an evening and chat with his neighbors over the fence. All this, in its manifold, inorganic patchwork, presents a picture of the uncurbed growth of the great city itself.

It is possible to make radical changes in prevailing conditions if we begin to plan carefully with the youngest children in the school garden, begin to explain, to demonstrate, and to educate. At first a unified garden-complex can be constructed into which the individual gardens are fitted as organic members. With certain quick growing groups of trees, with hedges, with border plantings along the main paths, wonders can be worked. A comprehensive division, by means of hedges, into garden areas, common playgrounds for children, and watering places, completes the picture. But it is necessary to insist upon the most careful preparation of compost, and the most sanitary disposal of refuse, as practiced, for instance, under the Bio-Dynamic method. Anyone who cannot adjust himself to composting, cannot keep his garden fertile and healthy; he damages it, and his neighbor's garden as well, through the spreading of diseases. Every garden settlement should maintain a model garden, in common, where composting, ideal plantings, intensive mixed cultures and herb plantings are demonstrated. School gardens could serve as prototypes and to teach the fundamental principles to the children. We should bear in mind, that just in the realm of landscaping the creation of something perfect consumes no more labor than the creation of a tinsely mess. The only essential is to make a communal, directed plan, which can be illustrated by means of models and demonstration layouts.

The following proposals have proven useful for the solution of such landscape problems in other parts of the world:

a) A uniform shape is recommended for the homestead gardens. They should be separated from their environment by hedges, shrubs, and groups of trees, and their value enhanced by a comprehensive, artistic plan. A plastic shaping, by means of grass plots, flower beds, springs, etc., acts as an effective example for the homesteaders.

b) The garden work should be guided in such a way that it leads to a biologically correct and soil conserving treatment of the land. The practice of composting should be encouraged, possibly by building communal compost heaps.

Indeed, communal compost yards are especially recommended when private heaps do not fit into the plans of the individual gardens. We suggest that the city's garbage removal department work with the city gardeners, and the responsible leaders of the home garden groups, for the purpose of arranging a communal

18

compost park where the valuable plant refuse of the city can be converted into humus. This compost economy can, through co-operation with the agricultural holdings in the homestead area, furnish the necessary fertilizer for the city projects in a refined condition.

A special monument should be erected in honor of city sanitation departments! In the environs of Paris there are gigantic heaps, upon which the total, unsorted contents of the garbage cans is piled up week in, week out. The heaps slowly smolder away, weather and decay, emanating unsavory odors. After years they yield a kind of compost earth of doubtful value. Often it is too tiresome for the farmer and gardener to wait until the fermentation is completed, and this half-decayed refuse is ploughed or spaded in. We have seen people working in a field where the potatoes had to be planted amid broken glass, bits of lead pipe, tar paper, garbage and old newspapers. Here we find the origin of countless infections, which start up in the slightest wounds, as well as the reason why Parisians are almost all afflicted with worms. A comparison should be made between the rate of tetanus in such regions and the rate in regions where a careful, selective composting is practiced.

In conclusion still another form of the home garden may be mentioned. This is a type which is customary on farms, and which lends itself to industrial homesteading projects in agricultural sections. On the farm the home garden area or vegetable plot is an integral part of the larger crop rotation. A strip of meadow or a clover field is ploughed and used for the garden for a few years. At the end of this period, manure is spread on it after the Fall harvest, and ploughed under. Thus it is caught up again in the normal agricultural crop rotation.

We should like to present as a model a farm belonging to a shoe factory, where this problem has been handled in exemplary fashion. The skilled craftsmanship needed in this factory calls for a resident supply of workers since frequent changes in personnel would not be economic. Only those workers who are permanently settled on the land can be considered truly resident. Included in this category are, of course, home owners who have gardens. The factory in question lies in the center of an agricultural area. The immediate landscape has a half-urban character, which is still quite rural on the outskirts. Since the original village straggled along one main road it still harbors stables and cattle. A great many of the workers, some of whom come from neighboring villages, have, in one way or another, a direct relationship to the soil. The rest live in little settlements and cultivate gardens. These gardens are, to a large extent, rented out by the company from its farm at a very low rate. At garden exhibitions the best home gardeners are awarded premiums by a community garden committee—for example, the land is made rent free. The home garden area still forms an essential part of the agriculture through the healthy interpenetration of the industrial settlement and the rural culture. It also takes part in the agricultural rotation. For some years it is a garden area and has the advantages of hand cultivation and compost fertilizing, but perhaps the disadvantage of a manure deficiency. Then it is turned back to agriculture and, by means of a crop rotation including legumes and manured crops, the probable deficiency is again compensated for. In the meantime, an adjoining field is converted into a garden area—and so on.[1]

[1] In *Bio-Dynamic Farming and Gardening* (Anthroposophic Press, New York, 1940), by the same author, general questions of soil fertility, soil cultivation, and landscape, as well as the Bio-Dynamic Method, are dealt with.

3. Home Garden Management

THERE IS little to be said about the size of the home garden. It is usually determined by local and personal circumstances. However, we will take a garden of at least 1080 square feet as the norm or average. Anyone who has a smaller area can cultivate it even more intensively according to the procedure described in Chapter V. An area larger than 54,000 square feet entails a great burden of labor, and cannot properly be counted as a home garden to be cultivated in our leisure time. Gardens beyond this maximum belong in the category of the small commercial garden from which surplus produce is marketed.

The following table shows the average yield of a small garden. Naturally, local conditions must be taken into account when using this table.

The Most Important Vegetables and Their Average Yield.

Tabulation compiled from experience with normal sized beds,
4 feet by 16½ feet.

Kind of Vegetable	No. Rows	Distance in Row	No. Plants	Yield in Lbs. or Pieces per Bed
Heavy Feeders:				
Cauliflower, early	3	2 ft.	24	24 heads
Cauliflower, late	2	2½ ft.	14	14 heads
Early Savoy Cabbage	3	20 in.	30	55 lbs.
Red & White Cabbage	3	20 in.	30	77-88 lbs.

Kind of Vegetable	No. Rows	Distance in Row	No. Plants	Yield in Lbs. or Pieces per Bed
Late Cabbage	3	2½ ft.	21	77-88 lbs.
Brussels Sprouts	3	2½ ft.	21	22-35 lbs.
Kale	3	2 ft.	24	45-55 lbs.
Kohl-rabi, early	5	9 in.	125	22-35 lbs.
Kohl-rabi, late	4	12-14 in.	60	30-45 lbs.
Leeks	5	6 in.	170	40-55 lbs.
Celeriac	3	20 in.	30	22 lbs.
Chard, Stem	2	16 in.	37	30-45 lbs.
Chard, Leaf	4	—	—	17 lbs.
Spinach	6	—	—	8-12 lbs.
Head Lettuce	4	10 in.	80	80 heads
Escarolle	4	16 in.	50	50 heads
Cucumbers	1	Hills	20	35-55 lbs.
Sweet Corn	2	20 in.	20	50 ears
Tomatoes	2	2 ft.	10	55-88 lbs.
Potatoes 8-12 lbs. seed for 324 sq. feet			100 pl.	110 lbs.

Light Feeders:

Carrots, early	6	Thinned	—	22 lbs.
Carrots, late	4	Thinned	—	22-44 lbs.
Beets	4	Thinned	—	35-44 lbs.
White Turnips, early and late	4	Thinned	—	35-44 lbs.
Early radishes as mark sowings	—	—	—	—
Winter radishes	5	Thinned	—	100 lbs.
Parsley and Herbs	5-6	—	—	—
Onions	5	5 in.	—	13-22 lbs.
Garlic and Shallots	6	3-5 in.	—	—

Plants which conserve and rest the soil:

Peas	2	(in hills or furrows)		11-17 lbs.
Bush Beans	4			17-22 lbs.
Pole Beans	2	2 ft.	15	132 lbs.
Shell Beans	3			11 lbs.
Lima Beans	4			15 lbs.

Every soil exhibits certain characteristics, such as inorganic and organic constituents, humus, degree of acidity, degree of weathering, nutritive content and fertilizer influences, the effects of climate, the condition resulting from previous cultivation, etc. These given factors must be taken into account when cultivating any soil. Cultivation can compensate for injuries and unbalanced conditions, for example, by aerating a heavy, wet soil. On the other hand, cultivation can be harmful if it is done carelessly or at the wrong time. Its influence is greater than the beginner or thoughtless gardener believes. Under given conditions, a 30% increase in yield can be achieved through the method of cultivation, alone.

We frequently hear deep cultivation recommended, particularly in connection with berry culture. The ground is worked to a depth of $1\frac{1}{2}$ to 2 feet, either with a spade or a trench plough. The object is to open up and aerate the subsoil with this deep cultivation, and to get rid of the roots of perennial weeds. Trenching by hand is time-consuming and therefore dearer in comparison than simply turning the soil with a spade. Since trenching which leaves the subsoil beneath and the topsoil above (the layers remaining undisturbed) is still more expensive, we often simply turn the soil structure upside down. What is the result? The topsoil, which had been aerated, enlivened, enriched with humus, is buried in a hole, with the solid, heavy subsoil now lying over it. Manure applied to such a soil, unable to decompose properly, cannot bring about sufficient improvement. We once saw a garden, part of which had been turned over in this way and the rest, for lack of time, had remained unspaded. We could mark off with a line that half of the garden where the unenlivened earth was on the surface making life difficult for the plants. Three years later the difference in favor of the untrenched land was still noticeable. People are in general too quick to trench plough, or turn a soil upside down. Such deep preparation should always be carried out so that the soil layers remain unshifted. Deep trenching is most essential where there is a hard-baked, clay subsoil, the drainage and aeration of which have been so hindered that they cannot be restored by other means. A healthy living soil will aerate itself from above and become ever deeper if it is given a soil-conserving crop rotation which includes the intensive cultivation of legumes.

In contrast to agricultural operations, gardening can be done almost entirely with hand tools. The beneficial effect of this upon the physical structure of the soil gives the gardener a great advantage.

Fall Cultivation.

Normally, we undertake deep cultivation of the soil only in the Autumn because the danger of drying out the soil is too great when this is done in the Spring. Fall ploughing and trenching encourage the penetration of Winter moisture. There is, of course, danger of erosion, but if we are turning sods, ploughing contour on slopes and have protective hedgerows, this danger is reduced to a minimum. Once the organic humus structure is established, there will be little danger of erosion. Even a brief frost period suffices to effect a fine crumbly structure of the soil. Simple spading also should be done in the Fall. All the garden beds should lie in rough clods over the Winter, except, of course, those planted with vegetables to be wintered over. A good dose of manure is advisable at the time of the Fall spading in preparation for the heavy feeding crops.

If humus compost and manure which have *completely turned into earth* are at hand, the fertilizer can be applied in the Spring. This is recommended in light, sandy soils. The spading should be done without breaking up the clods. The frost takes care of this far better, and aeration of the soil is secured. Weed roots should be carefully removed. This work pays for itself the whole year round. *Green, unrotted weeds should never be spaded under.* Before spading, the ground should be thinly peeled with a hoe or mattock and the weeds put on the compost heap. Green weeds and their decomposition in the ground attract wire worms and other soil pests.

Again, when grassland is first opened up, it is a good practice to cut thin sods with a spade or hoe and peel them off. Out of these the most superior sod compost can be made; at the same time the grub stage of the June beetle and other insect pests in the soil are destroyed. The top layer thus removed, is returned later in the form of the finest garden humus. Sod breaks down into compost very quickly, and can be improved by interlaying with manure.

A garden which has been spaded in the Fall should not be respaded in the Spring, as is frequently the custom. But it should be criled [1] or raked at this time and then immediately planted. Double spading merely blots out the good effects of the Winter soil decomposition.

Spring Spading and Ploughing.

When ploughing or spading is done in the Spring (for instance, on land where winter kale followed early potatoes), the clods should be broken up with a spade or fork and immediately smoothed out with a crile. It is advisable to spade only shallowly in the Spring, in order not to dry out the soil. If the weather is favorable everything should be carried out in rapidly succeeding operations in one day: cultivation, preparation of the beds and planting, that is, making the seed furrows, sowing, covering the furrows with good, ripe compost, firming the seeds so that they do not lie too loosely and have enough moisture for germination. It is better to complete one small piece of garden land in a day than to spade up a larger area and let it lie uncriled. In this way the danger and annoyance of a lumpy soil are avoided. All seeds

[1] A crile is a long-toothed tool known on the market as a round-tined potato hook.

prefer a freshly prepared soil. No subsequent watering can replace this.

A wet, heavy soil which has not been worked in the Fall should not be spaded in the Spring, but, if possible, simply cultivated with a crile. This corresponds to the agricultural experience that, contrary to the usual rule, better results are obtained in such a case from shallow ploughing.

Hoeing.

Once the plants have sprouted, hoeing should start immediately. Seeds which germinate slowly need a "marking seed" (for example, early radishes) so that the rows may be visible sooner. The moisture in a fresh, loose soil evaporates easily. In a loamy soil, because of the small spaces between the soil particles, it is sucked up to the surface like ink in a blotter. When the surface is broken up by shallow hoeing, the soil crust is destroyed, and, at the same time, the evaporation of moisture is checked. Three things are achieved by hoeing: the aeration of an encrusted soil, the destruction of weeds, which are more easily mastered at this initial stage, and the maintenance of soil moisture. At first the loosening of the soil must be very shallow, done, perhaps, by just pulling the hoe through it. Only later, after the roots have grown down to deeper soil levels, should the cultivation go deeper. Skillful and timely hoeing spares much watering.

Hilling.

Hilling is an important operation for the Summer months, helping peas, all types of beans, tomatoes and corn to gain firm anchorage in the ground. Furthermore, soil moisture is held around the roots of all cabbage varieties by this means. In light, dry soils hilling is indispensable for them, and, in all other types of soil, beneficial. Only kohl-rabi must be planted high, otherwise it stretches its stem out into length, instead of forming tubers. Leeks and finnochio are blanched by hilling up the soil around them. Tomatoes particularly reward a high hilling. They like to grow in a thoroughly warm and aerated soil. Since they have the faculty of forming roots on the stem above the crown, the root ball will be considerably increased by hilling. This means better nourishment for the plant as well as firmer anchorage in the ground. The same rules hold true for potatoes; here hilling is taken for granted.

An application of manure can be combined with hilling. Completely ripe, composted manure should be used, being drawn around the plants with a crile.

Something further must be mentioned here, which plays an important part in small gardens, especially in dry, sunny regions with light soils—for example, Southern New Jersey—namely, ground cover. It cannot be denied that the plants themselves, as soon as they have grown to some size, protect and shade the soil best, producing a soil fermentation which cannot be imitated. Indeed, herein lies one of the most useful effects of intercropping. However, until the interplanting is far enough along, we must help the little seedlings with an artificial ground cover, if we want to protect them from the various injuries brought about by too strong sunlight: drying out, crusting and washing of the soil. Half-rotted manure or straw compost forms the best ground cover or mulch for root crops and legumes. On the other hand, legume compost (or simply chopped pea or bean vines, cornstalks or straw) should be used for cabbages and the like. We covered late summer seedings of spinach as well as freshly set out brussels sprouts, for example, with the vines of just-harvested peas. An ideal mulch is formed by a mellow, not too wet, leaf compost. However, we need not despair if we do not yet possess such treasures. We have had no bad results from using hay, old grass, sting nettle straw and even shavings or grass cuttings. We must only take care not to mulch so thickly that the soil is made acid. Pine needles can be used to advantage for mulching strawberries and raspberries. They should not be raw, however, but should have been put through a composting process. It must be remembered, above all, that a dry soil, not to mention a baked out soil, is never mulched. Mulching after rainfall is best, on a cleaned and cultivated soil. The gardener will be delighted to find that hoeing and watering shrink to a minimum when he follows a careful mulching program. Then too, the weeds which force themselves through a mulch at least sit right loosely. Ordinarily, the mulch more or less disappears into the soil in the course of the growing season. By that time, however, the plants have matured and can take care of themselves.

Watering and Irrigation.

Watering should never be done, particularly in the case of a heavy soil, when it is not really necessary. The need for it should be limited by such measures as hoeing, hilling and mulching. If watering is necessary, the water used should, if possible, have stood for a time in the sun and air. Rain water is, of course, best of all. Furthermore, it is better to water seldom and thoroughly, than frequently and superficially! Otherwise the pampered plants develop only shallow, sprawling roots. Then if watering is once omitted, they suffer much more than plants which had learned long since to push their roots to deeper soil levels and search for water themselves. In hot, dry periods the garden should be divided into quarters. Perhaps once or twice weekly, according to need, each quarter should receive its generous share. The worried gardener need not kill himself lugging a watering can, although he must certainly water fresh sowings, young seedlings and some especially water-thirsty plants such as radishes and lettuce, every day. Cold sprayings with a hose under great pressure should always be avoided, as well as watering in full sunlight. During the Spring and Autumn, when the nights are cool, it is preferable to water in the morning. In the Summertime, when the danger of chilling the soil and plants is past, watering should be done in the evening in order to freshen them.

Tools.

One advantage man has over the animal is that instead of being dependent on a specialized form of claw or beak, he has been able to develop an extensive variety of tools to add to the efficiency of hand, foot and mouth. For the particular work of gardening there are many sorts of these tools, some much more useful than others. It pays greatly in time and effort to know exactly the right tool for each phase of the work. Every gardener develops preferences in the course of experience, so these suggestions are intended for the beginner, who may be bewildered by the variety from which a choice must be made.

When your tool list is ready try to get information from several sources, if possible. The highest price is not always the criterion for the best quality tool. An implement to be given hard usage, probably by several different persons, over a period of years, will prove more satisfactory if it is of the best quality, barring unnecessary decorative touches. Often lightness in weight is also an important feature of a well made tool and of particular interest if women are to be the users.

Power tools have little part in the small, intensive garden, yet if one also has other areas to cultivate and can afford the outlay for a Rototiller or garden tractor such as the Planet Jr. or the Gravely, it is a great help in the initial preparation of the garden area in each year's breaking of the soil.

Of greatest importance are the hand tools, for nothing can take the place of hand cultivation in the maintenance of a high degree of soil fertility. Procure some kind of hand wheel hoe, cultivator or garden plough, either with the large single wheel or the double wheel sort. These come with a variety of attachments. A Planet Jr. catalogue of farm and garden tools will give familiarity with representative varieties.

The shovel is usually preferred with a long handle, though it may also have the shorter "D" handle. This usually involves a difference in weight which is worth investigating. Why lift an added pound or two with each motion if lightness and strength can be combined?

A spade is less necessary than a four-pronged spading fork which does good service in digging out sod, and can also lift plants with less injury to the roots than a spade or shovel.

The bow head rake with 12 or 14 teeth is a more handy size than a wider one.

The very necessary and useful garden hoe has a number of valued relatives as well.

There is a "Gardex Rapid Hoe" with a patented swivel joint which combines weeding and cultivating efficiently and so that we need not walk on the soil that has been stirred.

The scuffle hoe will get into small corners where an ordinary hoe cannot function, especially against a wall or fence.

Another tool, a sort of cross between a hoe and a rake, is called by various names, including "crile," "speedy cultivator" or "potato hook". This is not effective in getting out unwanted roots—for that an ordinary hoe must be used—but it is the quickest tool for breaking the soil surface after a rain. With it the whole garden can be gone over in a short time, an important fact, since the crumbly surface so valuable in maintaining soil moisture can be gotten only if the job is done at just the right moment with the right degree of dryness.

These are the most essential hoes. A number of others such as the two-pronged weeding hoe, the Warren or heart-shaped hoe, the narrow nursery hoe, are good and may be personally preferred, but it is better to start with a few and learn all their possible adaptations.

Several small hand tools will be needed to use for transplanting, fine weeding and so on. A trowel of one piece steel blade and shank will give satisfactory service, whereas a cheap, thin one will soon bend and break at the base. One of narrow blade, often called the transplanting trowel, is convenient, as is also a finger

30

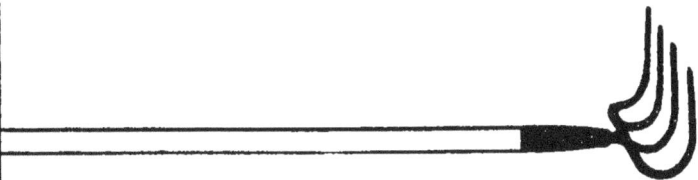

POTATO HOOK (CRILE)

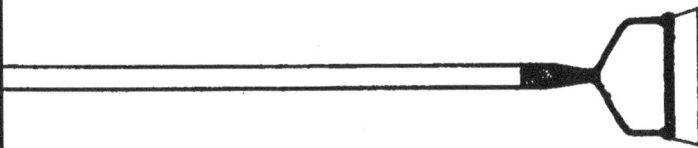

SCUFFLE HOE

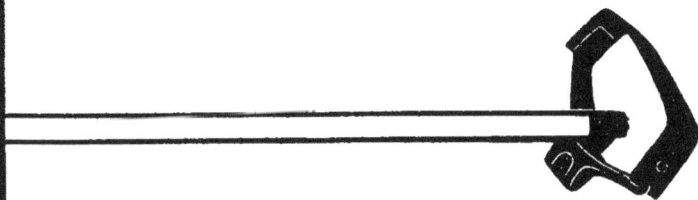

RAPID HOE

SPADING FORK

31

weeder. These come in various forms with from three to five finger-like, down-turned prongs on a short handle. A sharp and sturdy horticultural knife, in lieu of a good penknife, is a garden necessity.

In the small garden a sprinkling can may take the place of a garden hose, but is necessary in any case. Buy one of medium size—two to three gallons is ample and will not be too heavy when full.

Spraying on a small scale is best done with a bucket pump or a trombone type spray, also used with a bucket. These are not difficult to clean and are lighter weight, more easily handled combinations than the compressed air tank sprayers. A bucket is a necessity as well. The small pint or quart hand sprayers are insufficient for a garden.

Several baskets will be needed, from the ordinary bushel basket for collecting weeds, etc. to the basket with handle for gathering the harvest or carrying seedlings while transplanting.

Finally the wheelbarrow must not be forgotten. Here again weight is an important factor and probably the wooden barrow with removable side boards is the most generally useful.

When the array of new tools is finally assembled, it may be well to use bright colored paint to put an identifying band on each one. It is also very helpful to have a definite place to hang or stand each tool. If this is on a wall we can paint the shape of the tool just where it is to hang. Then a missing item is quickly noticed. To put away a used tool before it has been scraped clean and shining is said to indicate a poor gardener. In any case a clean, sharpened tool makes for much greater gardening efficiency. Especially in the late Fall when outdoor work is largely over, is it well to go over all tools, to clean thoroughly, oil the metal parts and if necessary paint the wood. Then we can take satisfaction in the possession, care and use of our fine tools and can feel that the season's work is well completed.

C. FERTILIZING.

When we consider the biological totality of the soil it is obvious that fertilizing feeds not only the plant, but the soil as well. The latter's life activity must be maintained. Nature provides for the bacteria, earthworms and roots with the humus content in the soil. Our first task, therefore, is to further the *organic* processes. The fertilizer must come to the soil in such a condition that it can fulfill this task. In this respect it is least effective when in a raw, fresh state. In such a case, biological energy and activity are consumed by its decay. It then lives on the soil for a certain time. The half-rotten products of decay (certain proteids, for example) are taken up directly by the plant roots and can work destructively in them. Well-known are the cooking odors of cauliflower and other vegetables—a direct proclamation of the kind of manure used.

The best form of organic fertilizer is humus. Unfortunately it takes a long time for stable manure to break down into humus. Meanwhile most valuable constituents disintegrate and are lost. For instance, the disintegration of nitrogen compounds takes place under the influence of certain bacteria. These bacteria are particularly active on the outer surface, that is, wherever there is enough air. When stable manure is carelessly tossed out and spread on the manure heap, and thus exposed directly to the rain and sun, up to 50% and more of its valuable nutritive substances is lost. What the sun does not leach out and oxidize is washed away by the rain.

If all the liquid gathers at the base of a manure heap, slowly "wetting its feet" and rising higher, then more and more air is excluded from the part standing in water or liquid manure and a correct fermentation is literally drowned. In that part of the heap a kind of peat-like, black, smelly mass is formed, with a very limited nutritive value. It smears the soil, breaks up poorly and after weeks we still find the black chunks almost unchanged.

Again, a too firmly packed manure runs the danger of becoming overheated and losing its best qualities through burning. Indeed there are many roads leading to a manure which has lost half of its original nutritive value. The alternative to following any of these is to turn at once to the *manure primer* and find out how a balance can be brought about.

The first and foremost rule is to set up the manure carefully from the first day onward. The initial step is to dig a pit of about a spade's depth, to which the manure is brought. Strawy, dry manure should be firmly trodden. If the soil is sandy the pit should be lined with a layer of straw. The practical form for a heap is a long rectangle. When the heap is completed it must be covered with earth. The earth which was taken from the pit can be used for this. The remainder can be obtained from a narrow ditch, about ½ spade deep, dug around the whole heap.

It is best to begin in one corner of the pit, building up a firmly trodden (but not trampled) section 20 to 40 inches high, 2 to 4 square yards in width. Next to this a second block should be built, a third, and so on.[2] By covering the first section with boards, the next can then be reached comfortably with the wheelbarrow. It is most important always to keep manure well covered. The action of those bacteria which break up the nitrogen compounds, ceases only when the access of air is considerably diminished. The best covering material is earth. A 2 to 3 finger thickness of a medium heavy soil is sufficient, and of heavier soils even less. This earth covering hinders washing and drying out. Only when no earth is available may peat moss, boards, straw, potato vines, etc. be used as substitutes. Heavy, loamy, clay soils, that is, impermeable soils, especially when wet, may be spread only in thin, scarcely finger thick, loose layers.

[2] We present a complete description of the care of manure intentionally. Although the home gardener, himself, does not usually take care of it, he should make sure that the manure he uses is of the finest quality and not a leached-out product. Our description enables him to evaluate it. If the stable manure is tested for nitrogen content, this evaluation is, of course, self-evident.

34

The heap should have just a boundary, or skin, to isolate it from the outer world. It should develop its own inner life. This life should not, however, run its course undirected, willy nilly, first here, then there. Only *one* definite direction is suitable to it and desirable for the farmer. The final goal for all healthy, organic decomposition is a neutral humus. Manure which has been led over to this condition offers the maximum in fertilizer value, both with respect to nutritive substances and physical structure.

The following short introduction is inserted for those interested in the Bio-Dynamic method. The practical application of the Bio-Dynamic method consists of a series of measures which, if carefully and conscientiously carried out, can lead to complete success. However, these measures require an enhancement of our observations of plant life. Those who approach them with mechanical habits of thought will not get very far. *To promote life* means to consider the manifold factors of the growing, ripening organism. The life of the plant world and of the soil in the field is not a mechanical process.

Some of the following instructions may seem non-essential to many people. They must remember, however, that only the combined activity of all these measures guarantees a maximum result. The efficacy of the bio-dynamic manure and compost preparations can be illustrated by the following. If we wish to make bread, we mix water and flour to a dough. This can then be left standing exposed to the air. Yeast bacteria (so-called wild yeast) present in the air, may accidentally settle on it and, in the course of some hours or days bring about a fermentation. The bread baked from this dough will be sour, bitter, hard, not edible. The baker, therefore, uses *one* special yeast culture or a "sour dough", in order to get a quick and good fermentation. The usual treatment of manure is comparable to the first instance—accidental fermentation. What should be attained, however, is a controlled fermentation which leads to a minor loss of nutritive substances and an improved humus formation. Dr. Rudolf Steiner indicated that such a desired activity resides in various plant preparations, and that these plant preparations are, accordingly, suited to lead the fermentation in the right direction. Experiments have shown that the preparations are also rich in plant hormones and growth stimulating substances.

What has been described in regard to the treatment of manure is also valid for the preparation of compost. Compost is a mixture of earth and all kinds of organic refuse which decomposes directly without having passed through an animal organism. However, it lacks the animal hormones, present in manure, which foster plant growth even when in very high dilution. In preparing compost something else must, therefore, be added. Already ripe earth, that is, earth containing bacteria and humus, should be added to act as a "ferment" or "sour dough". It is, therefore, advisable to leave a thin layer when removing an old compost heap and to build the new heap on this layer. Everything can be worked into a compost heap which will break down into humus. All kinds of plant refuse, straw, chaff from threshing, garbage, grass cuttings, even weeds (inorganic material, broken glass, tin, etc., should be carefully removed), ditch scrapings, street dust and muck, slaughterhouse refuse, horn, hoof and bonemeal, can be used.

The insertion of the bio-dynamic preparations Nos. 502-507 follows the covering of the heap. This procedure is the same for both manure and compost heaps and its purpose is to bring about a speedy, even decomposition, as well as to transform the organic products of decay into an odorless humus mass which can be quickly absorbed and digested by the soil. The individual preparations 502-506 are humus-like plant substances, gained, by a special process, from such well-known medicinal herbs as chamomile, yarrow and dandelion. Preparation 507 is an extract of valerian. Small portions of these preparations inserted in holes in large manure heaps, are sufficient to introduce a swift, healthy process of decomposition.[3]

When "preparing" manure and compost heaps, holes are made along the upper edge of the heap with a stick, at an angle toward the center, to a depth of about 2 feet. These holes run all around the heap, at yard intervals and, if the heaps are wide, also along the central ridge. Then about ½ to 1 ounce of each preparation (1 portion) is placed in each of the holes. If the heaps are small, three of the preparations can be put on one side and three on the other. With large heaps, either continue the holes or proceed as described above. Each hole receives a different preparation. Then the openings are again closed with earth after inserting the portions. Ten to twenty drops of the liquid preparation 507 are put in a gallon of water, making a solution which still has the valerian odor and is even slightly colored by it. The water used should be lukewarm and, if possible, rain water. The solution should be stirred for 10 to 15 minutes so that it is thoroughly mixed. A small part is then poured into the assigned hole, the remainder being finely sprayed over the whole heap. The rain water should not be boiled and then cooled, but merely warmed.

With the exception of cow manure, the exclusive use of *one* kind of animal manure ought to be avoided. It is preferable to mix the other types of manure with cow manure. Fertilizer for the production of the finest vegetables and fruits can be produced by composting manure. This can be done in two ways. Either the manure is interlayered with earth, or the manure layers are alternated with layers of half-rotted compost, and the mixtures allowed to stand for 2 to 4 months. Heaps of the latter type

---

[3] Details about the preparations and their effects can be found in *Bio-Dynamic Farming & Gardening*, by E. Pfeiffer, Anthroposophic Press, 1940, Chapter XI.

Further material appears in *Bio-Dynamics*, Vol. I, No. 1/2, published by the Bio-Dynamic Farming and Gardening Association, Inc. Phoenixville, Pa.

The activity of these preparations is connected with the currently much-discussed influence of growth hormones.

do not need to be turned. This method of composting manure produces a fertilizer excellent for certain special cultures. It is the best way to prepare pig, chicken, and rabbit manure. These are also set up in layers with earth or, if possible, with already half-rotted compost. This type of manure compost is best when worked in, later, after turning, with other kinds of compost. In any case, it is preferable to compost a one-sided manure rather than to plough it in as it is.

If we now inoculate a carefully set up manure heap with small portions of 502-507, the whole fermentation of this manure is directed to the formation of humus. After a short time, generally 2 months, the manure is changed into a brownish black mass rich in humus. Experiments have demonstrated that the bacteria content, during this process, is ten times that of an untreated heap.[4] The abundant earthworm activity is particularly striking. Such heaps immediately fill up with earthworms, which die, at the close of their humus forming activity, and yield additional fertilizer with their bodies. There are still a number of aspects of the problem to be considered, however, before we can be sure of achieving these results.

Strawy, loose manure overheats easily, especially when horse manure is present. Wet, fatty manure becomes putrid. The feeding program also has an influence upon manure production. The best manure is produced by coarse feed, grass eaten on the pasture, hay, clover, pea vines and other straw. Such manure has the most favorable structure for fermentation, especially when a great deal of straw bedding is used in the stable. Mangels, turnips, turnip leaves and exclusive green feeding in the stable produce too wet a manure. Concentrates also produce a manure with a wet, sticky structure which allows little air to penetrate it. The worst quality manure results from the exclusive feeding of concentrates, especially when leaves, sawdust, or peanut shells are used for bedding instead of straw.

[4] See table on page 53.

Experience has demonstrated that the decomposition of manure runs its course differently according to the base upon which it is heaped up. A better and quicker fermentation occurs on a humus and topsoil base, the slowest on a base of concrete. The action of the preparations is also quicker when the heap is set up on bare ground. With an earth base, a humus-like mass can be obtained within 4 to 8 weeks after preparing. The use of concrete bases should be avoided, if possible.

We shall now describe the ideal way to handle manure. De-

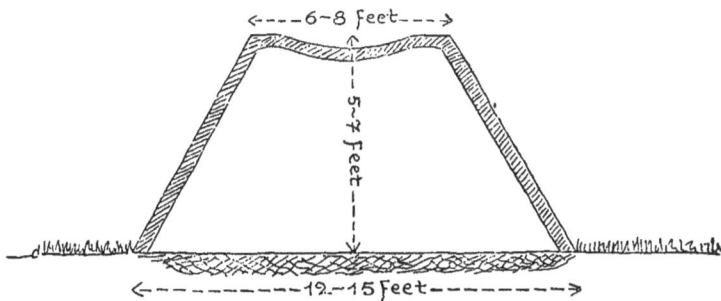

FIG. I.   SETTING UP AND COVERING A MANURE HEAP.

partures from the ideal are easily determined and can be adjusted to the fundamental rules. Since combinations of different manures work toward a better conservation of all their qualities (horse manure acts, for example, as a protection against denitrating bacteria), it is advisable to set up a mixed heap. Of course, if the horse manure is needed for hotbeds, it must be stored separately. The best procedure is to take the manure resulting from hay and pasture feeding, caught up in straw, and spread it out carefully over a small area of the manure yard. First make a layer of cow manure and cover this immediately with a thin layer of horse manure. The latter should lie open for some hours to steam out. Before the next stable cleanings are spread on the heap, the previous layer should be somewhat firmly trodden. If

39

the manure is strawy this can be done quite firmly, but if it is too wet and smeary treading must be omitted. Manure which is the product of concentrate feeding and contains little straw must lie open even longer to steam out, or to dry somewhat. When these blocks of manure have reached a height of, say, 3 to 3½ feet (strawy manure shrinks and can be built higher than wet manure, which sticks together in lumps when built too high) the heap is covered with earth, boards or straw. A covering for the side walls can be made of boards held together with pegs, which can be removed when the new block is set up alongside. When setting up long heaps successive sections of a yard in length should be completed and covered at once. These are then inoculated with the bio-dynamic preparations so that the fermentation can be guided in the right direction from the beginning.

Drainage must be provided for if the manure is too wet caused by the quality of the feeding, mixing with liquid manure, lack of bedding, or high rainfall. A manure heap must never "stand with its feet in the water". If manure is too wet it packs down more solidly, becomes fatty, and there is no longer enough air present for fermentation. When it is not possible to improve this condition by adding straw a system of drainage should be used to ventilate the heap. Brush from thorn bushes can be used for this purpose. If the heaps are exceedingly wet, or overheat easily, it may sometimes be advisable to arrange ventilation chimneys. These are then opened or closed as necessary. The liquid running out of the drainage canals is gathered in a tank at one end of the pit which should be sloped slightly in this direction.

Should the heap suffer from lack of air or get too hot, holes can be punched in it with a crowbar as an emergency measure.

The setting up of a compost heap proceeds in the following manner. The first step is to dig a pit for the heap, 5 to 10 inches in depth. If the subsoil is pure sand, it is best to line this pit with clay; ordinarily, a layer of straw is sufficient. If possible, a layer of already decomposed manure or compost is then spread over the new pit, or the bottom layer of the previous heap is left for a base. What has been said about the drainage and watering of the manure heap applies to compost as well. The structure and consistence of compost should also be moist but not wet. Alternate layers of compost material and earth are set up, always with a paper-thin layer of unslaked lime between. When a heap reaches a height of 4 to 6 feet it is covered with earth. The size of the heaps

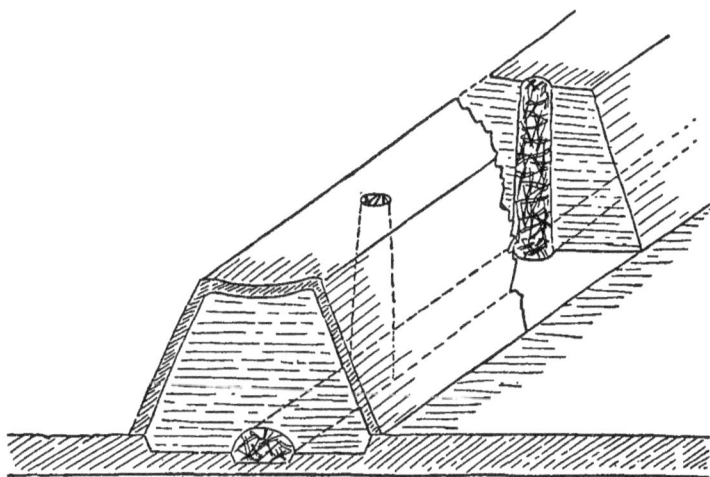

FIG. 2.   SKETCH OF A DRAINAGE SYSTEM FOR A MANURE OR COMPOST HEAP.

should be kept within the following bounds (or in the same proportion): length, as convenient; width at the top, 3 feet; height, 4 to 6 feet. First, then, comes a layer of plant material (approximately 2 to 4 fingers thick), then a paper-thin layer of unslaked granulated lime, then a layer of earth of 2 to 3 fingers thickness, then again a layer of plant refuse, quicklime, earth, and so on alternately. (The earth dug from the pit can be used for the inner layers, or road scrapings from untarred or unpaved roads—if such still exist—make good material.) If the covering earth is very sandy the sides of the heap should be made less steep so that it will not slide off. In a locality where frequent, strong winds occur, a protective covering of straw or reeds will be necessary. The top of the heap is shaped to a shallow trough. Water or diluted liquid manure for moistening the heap can be poured into this depression.

A compost heap can be built up gradually. This is necessarily the case if, for instance, the kitchen garbage from a small household is to be worked into the heap. In such instances, the sections must always be kept well-covered, say, with straw or rush mats.

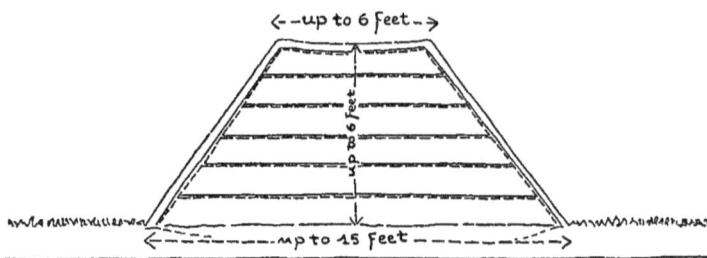

FIG. 3.   SETTING UP A COMPOST HEAP.

All kinds of weeds can also be used in the compost heap. However, these should be put only in the core of the heap. In this part, due to the lack of air, all the weed seeds are destroyed. When turning compost, the outside of the original heap should be made the core of the new, and the original core then becomes the new outside. This insures the destruction of the weed seeds in all parts of the heap. A compost heap should never be allowed to become overgrown with weeds. Grass, too, makes a thick mat with its roots and hinders decomposition. It is best to set up a separate weed compost and let it lie longer, even up to 5 months before turning and a year and a half before use. The normal rotting time of well handled compost, in a moist, cool climate, is from 8 to 12 months, for all sorts of compost material. Cabbage stalks, which need about a year and a half, are an exception. It is

42

preferable, therefore, to mix these with the weed compost. In the warmer climate of the South the time is considerably shorter, the minimum being about 2 months. Under such conditions, however, the covering and shading must be carefully done, otherwise the heaps will need to be watered frequently.

We have already mentioned that the appearance of earthworms in a manure heap indicates that the fertilizer preparations have begun to act. It must be added that this earthworm activity is greatly increased in a compost heap when onions or chicory are present. Then breeding places for earthworms immediately appear.

It is most essential that compost does not dry out. A compost yard should, therefore, be located in the shade of trees. If there are no trees some must be planted. There is no question that rotting takes place more quickly in half shade than in full sunlight.

Enclosing the compost yard with a hedge is also good, or, in the beginning, at least with a fence of straw or rush matting. In the home garden, sunflowers, sweet corn, or pole beans, can also be used for this temporary hedge. Elderberry, hazel-nut, alder and birch are particularly suitable for a permanent planting.

Dry manure and compost heaps require moistening or even watering. Dried out manure overheats easily. Fermentation ceases when moisture is no longer present, and the manure remains unchanged. At best, mould begins to form as a result of any chance wetting. This grayish-white growth, as well as the presence of wood lice in manure and compost, is always the sign of a too dry treatment of the material, and of overheating. The correct state of moisture for manure is that of a damp sponge; no liquid should run out of it, nor should it be stiff and dry.

In order to keep compost and manure in a moist state, it is helpful to pour a weak dilution of bio-dynamically treated liquid manure in rain water over the material while piling it. There are two kinds of liquid manure which can be used for this purpose. One is the liquid excretion of the animals, the other is made by dissolving pure cow manure in water. (Both should have been treated with preparations 502-507.) A crock can be kept at hand, in which to stir the second kind. The treatment of the compost heap with liquid manure, after it has been completed and prepared, is particularly important. Ordinarily a trough-like depression in the top of the heap is sufficient for its application. Water or liquid manure is poured into this trough and slowly seeps into the pile. In addition, some deep holes can be made toward the center of the heap. Then liquid manure is pumped over the heap as often as necessary, perhaps once a week. As it soaks into the pile it is absorbed by the organic matter present there. It does not become putrid, but is drawn into the general process of the fermentation. Its rank, harsh effect on plant growth is thus avoided.

If the heap has a peat moss cover this must be put aside before every application of liquid manure.

It is not necessary to drench the heaps with liquid manure or to pump torrents over them; moderate applications are sufficient. These, however, should take place regularly, alternating liquid manure with dissolved cow manure. Both are used in a dilution of I part to 12 to 15 parts of water, preferably rain water.

The preliminary treatment of the liquid manure, the preparing, may be described as follows. With it, as with manure, the *disappearance of the rank odor* is the characteristic sign of the effectiveness of the fertilizer preparations. The idea is to bring about as complete a fermentation as possible in order to soften the harsh effect of the liquid manure, and then to preserve this milder quality. It is necessary to stir it frequently, open to the air, so that the biological processes can develop quickly and well. These biological processes are especially furthered by the activity of the fertilizer preparations. It has been demonstrated that the fermentation takes place much more quickly in liquid manure pits lined with clay and covered with planks or logs than in cement tanks. Then too, a residue of old, fermented liquid, left in the pit, acts as a "leaven" for the newly gathered material and quickly starts the fermentation.

The same preparations, 502-507, are used for the liquid manure as for the stable manure. Preparation 507 is again stirred for a quarter of an hour in lukewarm water before application. It is then poured directly into the liquid manure. Preparations 502-506, however, are first placed in individual linen bags and fastened to a wooden cross, which floats on the surface of the liquid in the pit. The linen sacks themselves are submerged in the liquid manure, which should be stirred frequently. This wooden cross with the preparation sacks can be put in the liquid manure when it first gathers in the pit, even though the quantity may be small. The fermentation produces the best results only when the preparations can act for from 3 to 6 weeks without any new liquid manure being added to the pit. It is advisable, therefore, to divide the liquid manure container, or to plan two pits right from the beginning, so that the liquid manure added day by day can be stored separately from that which is to be prepared. The preparation of liquid manure has often been successfully accomplished by merely throwing the preparations in and then stirring them up—without using the floating wooden frame.

A manure barrel is of great value in the home garden for watering the compost. A small, strong barrel is half-buried (about up to the bung) in a semi-shaded spot. Earth is hilled up around the part above ground. The barrel is thus protected from rotting and a more even temperature is held in its contents. All kinds of manure which usually have a caustic effect when used alone (chicken, pigeon, and rabbit, for instance) are put in the barrel. This is then filled with water (rain water is best) and preparations 502-507 are applied as described above. Such a manure solution is particularly valuable for watering the growing or completed compost heap. It should also be diluted with water in the same proportion as liquid manure. The water in the barrel is replenished from time to time, and the solid manure thus gradually used up. The occasional addition of more manure is therefore necessary.

Usually, a manure which has been carefully set up and given the bio-dynamic preparations becomes ripe in *two months,* is transformed into a humus-like mass ready for use. If disturbances are evident in the fermentation, such as putrefaction, mould formation, or overheating (due to dryness, wetness, or an excess of one type of manure) then it is advisable to turn the heap. This can be done, when necessary, from the second month on. If the fermentation has already changed the heap into an odorless mass,

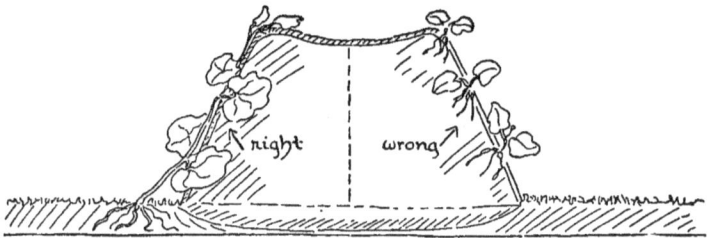

A. CORRECT   B. INCORRECT
FIG. 4. CORRECT AND INCORRECT PLANTINGS FOR A COMPOST HEAP.

after two months, turning is unnecessary. When a heap, which is being turned, seems to be too dry and to have too high a temperature (anything over 150° Fahrenheit must be considered harmful), it must be thoroughly watered. Turning on a rainy day is indicated. In dry summers we observed a different rate of decomposition on the north and south sides of the heaps. In general manure and compost decompose more quickly on the shaded side.

After about two months compost has an earthy quality. All unpleasant smelling substances have disappeared and it has a humus odor which is reminiscent of woods earth. The presence of many earthworms is a sign that the heap is ready to be turned.

46

However, the best and most carefully cared for fertilizer can exercise no effect on plant growth, if it is dug into the soil so deeply that its further decomposition more nearly approaches a process of peat formation than one of rotting. This can easily occur in tough, heavy soils. The manure should be worked into the soil as shallowly as possible, so that the process of decomposition which goes on in the ground can take a favorable course and the best possible effect be obtained from it.[5] An uncared for, raw, that is, not sufficiently decomposed fertilizer will not infrequently have a harmful influence upon the soil. It can even cause reductions in yield.

The following points must still be considered. Processes of fermentation leading to the formation of humus proceed very slowly when the temperature nears the freezing point and when the material used is very dry. There is, therefore, not much sense in making a compost heap in Winter, if the material is cold or frozen. It is also difficult to bring about decomposition in dried out material during a dry Summer. In such a case, we can help by wetting the material while setting it up. We should also take care to maintain the moisture of compost and manure heaps during periods of drought.

We once saw a leaf compost which after a year showed no sign whatever of decomposition. What had happened? The leaves, having fallen the previous Winter, had been raked together dry and set up in Midsummer. They were already baked together in clumps and then were set up in fairly thick layers. No air or moisture could penetrate this mass. The edges of the layers had broken down, but the leaves in the center lay there just as when set up. Leaf compost should be heaped up in Autumn immediately after the leaves have fallen. We should rake the leaves over well and toss them up, make thin layers, and take care that the whole is really moist.

At another time we saw a compost heap which did not rot, al-

[5] See also Chapter V on the cultivation of vegetables.

though it had been correctly handled in every detail. The earth used in the inner layers of this heap came from a vineyard which had previously been treated intensively with copper sprays. The earth was sterilized and the bacteria necessary for decomposition had been killed off. We must, therefore, be careful to use *healthy earth,* and not earth that has been saturated with one chemical or another (copper, lead, arsenic, nicotine). Even the smallest quantities of these substances are known to be hostile to bacteria.

The condition of the manure or compost at the time of turning determines whether it is necessary to insert the fertilizer preparations again or not. Usually decomposition will have gone so far that the layers are no longer visible. Naturally a relayering of the material is not necessary when turning it. Since the individual heaps may have shrunk considerably, two heaps can be turned together into one.

If the original heap contained weeds or leaves which were infected with fungus diseases, we must be careful, when turning it, to make the outer part of the old heap the core of the new one, and vice versa. Seeds and pests are destroyed in the inner part of the heap due to the lack of oxygen. It is thus possible to avoid resowing the weed seeds with the compost.

Anyone who delves deeply into the making of compost will soon make two discoveries. He will first find that compost making is an art. Then he will be astonished to see how much compost he gets if he carefully collects all the refuse on his place. It is always much more than he would have believed possible.

We come now to the preparations 500 and 501, so many-sided in their application. These are dissolved in water and finely sprayed, directly on the soil (500) and on the green leaves (501). When we speak here of sprays, it should be carefully noted that we do not mean the poisonous, chemical sprays used for fighting pests. The materials discussed are substances, such as manure and quartz, which have been made biologically active through a special process. Both sprays (500 and 501) have no actual fertilizer

48

effect in the sense of strong doses of a nutritive substance. However, both have a dynamic, that is, a growth-stimulating effect. Their presence, even in the high dilution still to be described, causes definite changes in plant life.

500, the preparation consisting of specially treated manure-humus, is connected with all the processes which have to do with *germination, root formation*—all the processes in the soil. It is, therefore, applied at all times when these processes are to be especially directed or fostered. In a similar way, *501* directs all the processes which have to do with growth in length, the further development of the plant, and especially the processes of assimilation which take place in the green parts of the plant above the surface of the soil.

The intimate student of plant life who has familiarized himself, through living observation, with the three chief stages of plant growth—germination and root formation, development of leaf, stem and blossom, and the formation and ripening of the fruit—will be able to judge when to apply both of these preparations. The greatest effect can be achieved only by spraying at the correct time. It is also possible thus to influence the quantitative yield.

In general 500 is applied in the Spring and Fall and is sprayed directly on the ground, either *before sowing* or before Fall cultivation. If it is sprayed before sowing or during planting (more detailed instructions are given in Chapter V), it should be worked into the soil with a crile or rake immediately after its application. Since it stimulates root growth and germination, as well as the formation of humus (that is, all organic processes in the soil) it is understandable that it must *penetrate* the soil to be effective. If possible, therefore, it should not be applied to a completely dried out, crusted, hardened soil. Spraying 500 toward evening has proved to be particularly effective, since it is then absorbed by the soil with the falling dew. On the other hand, spraying during rain or immediately afterward, or in the full sun at mid-day, should be avoided.

Garden culture represents a more intensive treatment of each square yard of land in contrast to field culture. It follows, therefore, that the preparations are also used more intensively in the garden. For instance, spraying the planting furrow or hole with 500 before transplanting, or at least dipping the plant roots in this solution, is recommended. This is also valuable for trees. When setting out trees it is important, too, to put good, well-rotted compost in the planting holes. In the small intensive garden, early potatoes can be planted in a trench which has been lightly sprinkled with compost and sprayed with 500.

Stirring and Spraying Preparations 500 and 501.

One portion of 500 (about 40 grams or 2 ounces) is dissolved in 2½ gallons of lukewarm water. Rain water is best. The container must be of wood or earthenware. A galvanized pail should never be used, save in an emergency. Stir the solution with a short stick or birch branch, in one direction, vigorously enough to form a deep funnel, but not so vigorously that it splashes out. (Use a large enough crock!) Then reverse and stir in the same manner in the opposite direction until another funnel appears. Again reverse the direction and repeat this alternation for *one* hour. Long years of experience have demonstrated that it is very important for the effectiveness of the preparation that this procedure be carried out as exactly as possible and for *one hour*.

The preparation should be applied as soon as possible after stirring. Experiments carried out at the Research Laboratory at the Goetheanum (Dornach, Switzerland) show that the solution has the strongest effect when sprayed on the ground within 3 hours after stirring. Later it loses strength, and, if left standing over night or longer, becomes useless.

Preparation 501 is made of quartz (preferably mountain crystal) which is "activated" by the process through which it is put. A portion of this material (½ to 1 gram equals a portion) stirred in 2½ gallons of water is sufficient for one acre. This preparation manifests the *dynamic* effect to a particular degree. (Compare here the article in No. I and II of *Bio-Dynamics*.) It must also be stirred for *one hour* and then sprayed as soon as possible, as described in the case of 500. However, it is sprayed on the plants and should be more finely distributed, in a kind of mist. A pressure spray of the type used in orchard culture is therefore best suited to the application of 501. This must be kept painstakingly clean and should *never* be used for arsenic, lead, or copper compounds.

Because of the effect which preparation 501 has on the life processes in the green plant parts, it is applied only to the already *developing* plant. It should not be used in Spring as long as there is still danger of night frosts, except on cultures growing in very sheltered spots. Usually the spraying of 501 can begin in the month of May. As soon as the roots of the plants are well established, the young leaves have unfolded and the weather promises quick growth, the first spraying can be made. A second application can follow in 2 to 4 weeks. In particular, 501 promotes the leaf and stem growth prior to blossoming. No preparation may be applied to blossoming plants. Naturally fruit trees, which flower before their leaves come out, receive 501 only after they have blossomed.

This preparation has a kind of "balancing effect" on plant growth. For instance, retarded, too slow growth is stimulated, too rank and swift a growth slowed up. 501 should be used *more frequently in wet years,* therefore, when plants are apt to shoot up too quickly. It should not be applied to young fruit trees in the first years, especially if the trees are still to be transplanted or grafted. Again, 501 must not be applied to annual plants *before* transplanting.

An important rule to be kept in mind is that 501 may not be used unless 500 has previously been applied. Its full effect can only develop if this is the case.

Those who have worked intensively with the preparations for

51

some years will be able to devise special applications and combinations for themselves. Since these conform to local conditions, to the type of culture, to the weather, etc., they cannot be discussed in detail here. However, one example may be given.

At a certain stage in their growth broad beans are attacked by plant lice. When the plants grow larger the lice disappear. If we bring the plants quickly past the critical stage,· by stimulating their growth, they may thus be protected from the attack of lice. Applying preparation 501 after the appearance of, say, the fourth leaf will help in this case.

Sprays.

The longer we practice the Bio-Dynamic method, working thus to restore balance in nature, the less troublesome insect pests become. This becomes evident in proportion to the size of the area where the method is in use. With an isolated small garden,.we may have more difficulty because our neighbor's pests will be forever flying, hopping or burrowing into our territory.

We avoid the use of poisonous sprays whenever possible. But if a crop is endangered, then we prefer to use sprays made out of plant materials rather than those of chemical origin. Besides the danger to human beings of spray residue on foodstuffs, many chemical sprays, made up of arsenic, lead and copper compounds, are harmful because of the metallic residues left in the soil, these often remaining there for years, where they prevent the normal development of all kinds of soil organisms. Careful experiments have shown that although the plant sprays are no less harmful to earthworms and bacteria, they disintegrate within a few days, doing no permanent damage to the soil. Even these, however, *should not be used on any vegetable or food plant less than three weeks* before they are to be eaten.

The following materials may be used against various insect pests, each according to the directions which come with it:

derris, containing rotenone, as spray or dust,
pyrethrum,
nicotine mixtures such as Black Leaf 40,
quassia and soap solution.

In estimating the manure and compost needs of the home garden we can reckon on 4 pounds of manure and 6 to 8 pounds of compost per square yard, annually. These are either applied separately or mixed together.

We should like to present the following table before concluding this discussion of fertilizer needs and values.

Manure Analysis

Bacteriological findings:

	Aerobic Bacteria	Anaerobic Bacteria	Total
Fresh manure	34.8 mill.	56.56 mill.	91.36 mill.
Manure, six months old	44.0 mill.	29.12 mill.	73.12 mill.
Bio-dynamically treated, four months old	702.32 mill.	417.6 mill.	1119.92 mill.

Chemical findings:

	B-d. treated 4 mos. old	Non B-d. 6 mos. old	Proportionate Value
Water content	21.713%	31.516%	——
Organic matter	10.540%	7.164%	1.5 : 1
Ammonia	trace	0.118%	——
Nitrogen, inorganic (nitric acid)	0.052%	0.003%	17 : 1
Nitrogen, organic	0.823%	0.130%	6 : 1
Phosphoric acid	0.255%	0.171%	1.5 : 1
Potassium	1.069%	0.539%	2 : 1

This analysis is instructive in many respects. In the first place, it points out the considerably heightened bacterial activity in the bio-dynamically treated manure. Secondly, it describes the transformation which took place during treatment, since both manures are from the same source. The table shows that, with the bio-dynamic treatment, less substances are washed away during the decomposition (potassium and phosphoric acid), and that nitrogen and organic matter are retained; while, in the other case, they have left the manure in the form of ammonia and carbon dioxide. (Compare the proportionate value of the two manures.) If we now consider that the water content of the bio-dynamic manure is 10% less than that of the untreated (which means considerably less water to be hauled out onto the field), it is evident where true fertilizer value can be found.

D. HOTBEDS AND COLDFRAMES.

Does the home gardener need a hotbed? This question can be answered both affirmatively and negatively. In the garden itself there is really no proper place for it. Hotbeds and coldframes must always be under the gardener's eye—as near the house as possible. They require constant attention and a certain amount of skill and experience. The beginner had better give up the idea of having a hotbed for some years, until he has a general grasp of other work and acquired some dexterity. Later on, a hotbed will be of value, not only because it produces his own seedlings and early lettuce and radishes, but also because of the manure-earth which he can get from it. Manure-earth is the finest of all compost earths, even better than good rotted stable manure.

A hotbed or coldframe layout should be protected on the weather side by, for example, a hedge or a stable wall. A fence of matting can be used for temporary protection. The area should be open toward the south or southwest.

A smooth, clean pit about 2 feet deep is dug, corresponding in length to the number of sash to be used. The width must of course correspond to the length of the sash. Neither stony ground nor an area with a high ground-water level are suitable for the location of frames.

The next step is to make a frame out of good strong boards

(about one inch in thickness). This frame is anchored at the corners with stakes and braced at the width of the sash with smaller cross pieces. The glass is laid on a slight slope, to let the rain run off and to absorb the light and warmth of the sun. The back wall of the frame should be 10 to 12 inches above ground and the front wall five or six. Hardwood must be used for these frames since preservatives are harmful to plants. Although concrete frames are nearly imperishable, they are not good. The temperature variations in concrete frames are much too abrupt and therefore harmful. Wooden frames insure much better health for the plants. On the other hand, metal sash with one center brace and few single panes make the best cover. Wooden sash are very heavy. The most manageable size for sash is 3 by 4½ feet.

For purposes of forcing, the frame is packed with warm horse manure in February and March, and, when possible, the outside walls heaped around with manure. A sunny day should be chosen for the packing. Careful building up of the manure layers and treading are important. A layer of straw or a thin layer of leaves is first spread over the bottom of the pit to insulate the manure from the frozen ground. For a very warm packing, a 1½ to 2 foot layer of manure is made, though ordinarily a 1 foot layer is sufficient. An intermediate layer of rotted leaves and a light covering layer serve to equalize the warmth. The addition of more leaves gives a cooler packing. After 3 to 5 days, when the manure is well warmed through, earth is spread over it to a depth of 6 inches. It is then necessary to wait 2 more days, before sowing, until the earth has settled somewhat and is thoroughly warmed. The earth used in hotbeds should be ripe, fine in texture and not too heavy. About 6 inches of air space are left between the glass and the seeding.

The gardener must be consistent in caring for hotbeds and coldframes. Aside from watering they require careful ventilation and shading. There are also straw mats which are used for covering when extra warmth is necessary and must be removed again when the outside temperature rises. A great deal of experience is necessary in order to do these things correctly and this is only gained from long observation of the plants and beds. In late Spring the plants should be gradually hardened. At first the ventilation is increased, then the sash are left off during the day and finally removed altogether.

Forcing vegetables are grown in hotbeds and the seedlings of early kohl-rabi, lettuce, cauliflower, celeriac, tomatoes, leeks and onions are raised in them. Coldframes are used principally for starting the later varieties of cabbage. Later in the season, the less delicate vegetables are sown in the open in well prepared seed beds.

The bio-dynamic preparations are also used in hotbeds and coldframes. In fact, preparation 500 is always lightly raked into the carefully leveled beds before sowing. Should the temperature in a hotbed begin to drop, then preparations 502-507 are inserted. This is done by punching holes through the earth layer with a rake handle, as in preparing a compost heap. The remainder of preparation 507 is sprinkled lightly over the bed. Preparation 501 is not applied to seedlings before they are set out in the garden.

Movable coldframes are especially valuable on a small place. This is a type of glass culture widely in use in Europe. The wooden frames are of light construction, so that they can be moved from bed to bed. The sashes are smaller than those commonly in use in the United States, thus easier to handle. (The standard size used here is 3 by 6 feet, in contrast to 3 by 4½ feet, the usual size for the portable sash.) These portable frames can be set over the garden beds in the Spring to protect certain cultures and force them somewhat (for example, spinach, radishes, etc.). In the Fall they can be used to ripen bush beans, carrots, etc. There are countless ways of using movable frames. During the summer months, for example, tomato houses can be made out of the sash. A skillful gardener uses them the whole year round so that he scarcely finds time for necessary repairs.

Suggested Uses for Portable Coldframes

JANUARY: Spinach, corn salad.
FEBRUARY: Spinach, corn salad, radishes.
MARCH: Carrots, head lettuce, possibly early peas, radishes.
APRIL: Lettuce, kohl-rabi, bush beans.
MAY: Bush beans, tomatoes.
JUNE: Cucumbers.
AUGUST-NOVEMBER: Temporary house for tomatoes and bush beans.
DECEMBER: Spinach, corn salad, parsley for cutting.

They can also be used for wintering over various vegetables. (See Chapter V.)

Note:

To simplify the use of several individual preparations, the Bio-Dynamic Compost Starter was developed by E.E. Pfeiffer. It contains the preparations and additional bacteria cultures.

He wrote: "It would be ignoring scientific progress if we were not to invistigate the use of bacteria culture especially suited to the purpose. Those familiar with fermentation in science and industry know very well that controlled fermentation works economically and successfully to produce end material excelling in quality. The B.D. Compost Starter will decompose all organic matter and is not harmful to living organisms. It should also be noted that bacterial action will not be impaired by cold and frost."

For more information contact:

The Pfeiffer Foundation
Threefold Farm
Spring Valley, N.Y. 10977

4. The Crop Rotation and the Significance of Mixed Cultures

IN THE FOREST, in the meadow, in every wild plant association, there is a colorful mixture of plants, which, in accordance with the soil type and local climatic conditions, are able
to live together and mutually complement one another. We often
speak of a "natural plant association". The substances resulting
from the decomposition of the plants, the excretions of the animals and all decaying organic matter, care for the formation of
natural humus, which is held fast by the roots of the plants and
utilized by them. The plants in many regions associate in such a
varied manner, that blossoms, green leaves and fruits hang next
one another, at every season, up to the time of killing frosts.

A secret life then hides itself in the subterranean rootstocks,
bulbs and tubers of the perennial plants, in the slumbering eyes
of the trees and shrubs. It lies there ready to push forward again
with the increasing warmth of Spring and manifest itself anew in
growing and blossoming.

The conditions are quite otherwise in cultivated land, in the
field and garden. Here, in the course of *one* period of vegetation,
plants are cultivated which for the most part do not even become
completely ripe, aside from grain and certain fruits. They are sup-
posed to develop the greatest possible leaf mass, as, for example,
cabbage and spinach, or, as in the case of turnips, to form large
roots. The plant thus makes great and often truly one-sided demands on the soil. Cultivation of the soil and fertilizing are therefore necessary, the first to aerate and open up the soil, the second

58

to supply nutritive substances and maintain a balance. The plants must alternate with one another in a succession which uses the ground without robbing it, and lets it rest again at intervals, so that it is not made one-sidedly poor in nutritive content. This means that we must use a crop rotation such as will be described.

In horticulture plants are classified according to their requirements and their more or less one-sided utilization of the food substances in the soil. They may thus be divided into heavy feeders, light feeders, soil conserving and soil improving plants. All plants which need a heavy fertilizing with stable manure are *heavy feeders*. They can also utilize applications of liquid manure. Entirely fresh, untreated manure or liquid manure are not used, however, even for them. The heavy feeders are planted immediately after fertilizing. We speak of them as belonging in the "first rank". The most familiar heavy feeders are all the cabbage varieties, cauliflower in particular, all leaf vegetables such as chard, head lettuce, endive and spinach, as well as celery and celeriac, leeks, cucumbers, squash and sweet corn.

Rhubarb and tomatoes are also decidedly heavy feeders, but are not included in the crop rotation since rhubarb is a perennial and special rules apply to tomatoes. (See cultural instructions.) Berry bushes and strawberries likewise require a rich, but not a fresh manure.

The heavy feeders can be followed by legumes. To these belong pole beans, peas, sugar peas, broad beans, shell beans, lima and soya beans. They bring about the recovery and improvement of the soil which has been depleted by the heavy feeders. By means of their deep growing roots legumes open up lower soil levels and bring nutritive substances which may have been washed down (lime for instance) to the surface again. The roots of many annual legumes reach to a depth of 2 feet; perennial types go even deeper, alfalfa and sainfoin reaching a depth of $6\frac{1}{2}$ feet in a deep soil. By means of the nodule bacteria on their roots all the legumes capture the air's free nitrogen. In this way they provide for necessary nutritive materials and produce supplementary fertilizer.

In a very run-down soil, we should always put the legumes in the "second rank" and plant them directly after the heavy feeders. In a live humus soil they can remain in the "third rank", in which case a light compost fertilizing benefits them.

It would really be more appropriate to call the *light feeders* "compost lovers". They cannot stand heavy fertilizing with strong stable manure or fresh manure, which cause a rank, coarse growth. Instead, they should be fertilized with good compost. We are dealing here with bulbs and all root vegetables, such as carrots, beets, radishes, etc. They stand to best advantage when placed in the "second rank".

Annual and perennial aromatic herbs help to conserve the soil and "enliven" the vegetable garden, which blossoms relatively little. These, also, can stand only compost fertilizing.

There are still some plants to be mentioned, which, because of the peculiar character of their growth, their scent and their root formation and soil demands, have a beneficial effect upon the garden. These can be used for border plantings. We are thinking here, chiefly, of sweet corn, sunflowers and hemp, which form a good annual hedging for the garden. Despite the fact that they make strong demands on the soil, they can be considered biologically useful plants. Because of its peculiar odor, hemp[1] acts as a deterrent on the cabbage butterfly. This is very useful in the flight years of this butterfly. Sunflowers attract the tomtits, which then proceed to hunt grubs and insects. Bees also enjoy visiting them. If we allow the herbs in our garden to go to seed the bees and all kinds of useful insects have a great feast while they are in blossom. Blossoming hyssop, thyme, savory and borage form a good, healthful bee pasture.

The fine root structure of flax has an excellent soil loosening effect. Carrots are especially grateful for such a soil. Besides flax,

[1] Unfortunately hemp cannot be planted in many states because of misuse.

PLANTING PLANS OF A SECTION OF THE INTENSIVE GARDEN FOR THREE SUCCESSIVE YEARS

Sunflowers   Strawberries   Chives   Red Radish   Cauliflower   Ka Kale, Cabbage
Pole Beans   T Tomatoes   Parsley   L Lettuce   On Onions   R Romaine Lettuce
X Sugar Corn   Pumpkin   Carrots, Turnips   Peas   Corn Salad   Cu Cucumber

Compost

Spring

Aftercrop

First Year

C Early Cabbage   Ⓑ Beets   Ᏸ Early Radish   B Bush Beans   S Spinach
Ꝼ Brussels Sprouts   Sq Squash

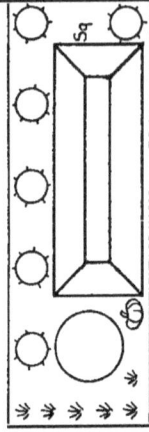

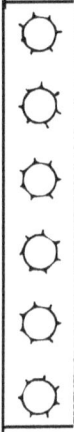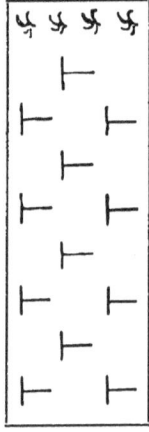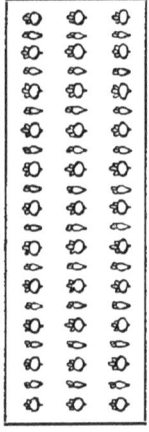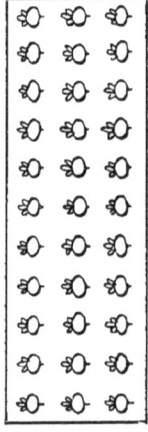

Spring

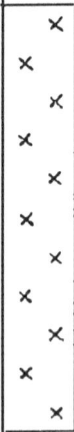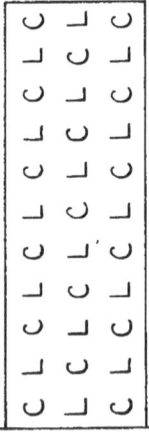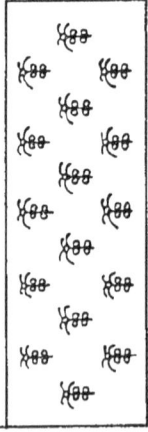

Aftercrop

Second Year

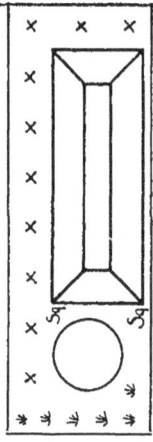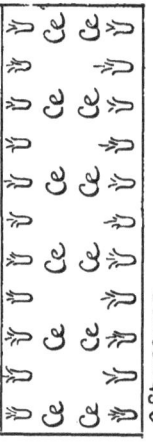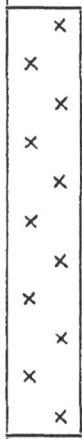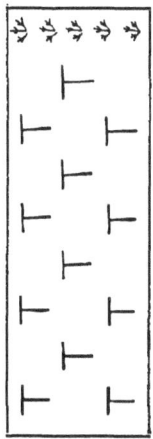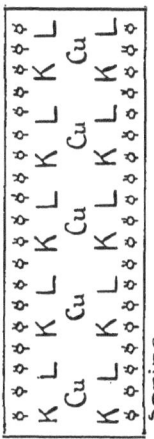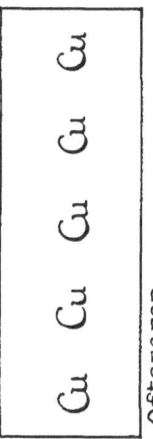

K Kohlrabi E Escarole ⚘ Dill ♂ Summer Radish ϒ Leek Ce Celery Cu Cucumber

Spring Aftercrop

Third Year

soya beans and lupins are the plants which leave behind them the finest, most friable soil.

It is not a matter of indifference in what associations plants are grown. We need only think how the shallow-rooting and deep-rooting plants supplement one another through the differentiation in their root systems. The legumes, for example, promote root growth in their neighborhood through the aeration of the soil resulting from their own deep-growing roots. It has been observed that beets and kohl-rabi grow very wretchedly near pole beans, if planted too late and consequently shaded by the beans. Between cabbages they thrive well, even in a very cramped and heavily shaded position. Another unfavorable combination is tomatoes and kohl-rabi. If they are planted together, the one planted last generally suffers. Similarly, fennel and tomatoes cannot stand one another. While we value sunflowers as a border planting, along a path, a lane, or a meadow, it is not good to plant them near potatoes. We run the risk of having stunted vines and small potatoes, especially if the sunflowers develop luxuriantly.

Cabbage and beans, beets and onions, celeriac and leeks, cucumbers and sweet corn are counted among mutually beneficial combinations. (Corn can be used as a border planting or may be planted in a neighboring bed.) Beans are also not harmful when planted in the immediate neighborhood of celeriac and leeks. However, if we plant beans too thickly between celeriac and leeks, all three are generally stunted. Further beneficial associations are carrots and peas, cucumbers and beans, kohl-rabi and beets, onions and beets, early potatoes and corn, early potatoes and beans, early potatoes and horseradish (the latter as a border), tomatoes and parsley, bush beans and celeriac, cucumbers and bush beans. A harmful association is fennel and bush beans. There is still much to be investigated in the field of plant symbiosis. We would like, therefore, to urge that the gardener observe and note his own experiences for future reference.

The sense of companion cropping now becomes clear. Above the soil as well as under it, the neighboring plants supplement one another. For example, the upward striving, two-dimensional leek finds enough room near the bushy celeriac plant. Both are potassium lovers and prefer, therefore, well-rotted pig manure. The intercropping of various plants is conditioned by their similarity in soil demands and difference in rate of development. Lettuce and kohl-rabi, for instance, have short seasons of development and cover the ground as long as the plants which mature later cannot yet do this. After the inter-crop is harvested the later maturing plants remain with plenty of room in which to develop.

Mixed cultures not only give the advantage of a permanent ground cover, which prevents crusting and drying out, but also help to hold the weeds in check. Besides, they have a marked influence on the quality, keeping quality, and flavor of the vegetables. We suggest the following simple experiment as a test of the validity of the preceding statement. Plant 2 or 3 rows of radishes and beside them 2 or 3 rows of garden cress; in a second plot, nearby, use chervil as a border; then, lastly, plant a few rows without a border, as a control. You will be able to detect marked differences in flavor:

Radishes without a border: relatively tasteless.
Radishes with a border of chervil: sharp.
Radishes with a border of garden cress: very tasty.

5. Vegetable Production Concentrated on the Smallest Area

THE ORDINARY, flat garden bed is not used for this kind of concentrated vegetable production, but the land is arranged in waves or ridges, which somewhat resemble long-cultivated asparagus beds. However, not just a single crop is grown, but all the vegetables necessary to the household are planted on the crests of the ridges, on the sides and in the troughs, in a well thought out combination and rotation. No paths are laid out. After every harvest the area left open is at once newly sown or planted. As a result of the necessary intensive cultivation and the ground cover afforded by the plants themselves, as well as the aeration and enlivening of the raised soil level, an excellent soil structure is achieved. Soils which tend toward acidity and do not respond to applications of manure can be improved in this way.

Such a soured soil was chosen for our first experiment. We prepared a piece 16½ feet long and 11 feet wide. This was divided into 4 ridges and 3 troughs along the shorter side. In practice it proved better to make somewhat wider troughs in order to have room to step around among the plants. The wider troughs facilitate cultivation and harvesting. This garden was first planted in 1938. From this area, of slightly more than twenty square yards, the following were harvested:

Spinach	5.291 lbs.		Kohl-rabi	45 pieces
Beets	61.728 "		Lettuce	240 heads
Corn Salad	1.984 "		Winter radishes	60 pieces
Celeriac	14.903 "			
Celery	3.527 "			
Lupin seeds	1.102 "			

66

The lupins were planted in order to improve the soil. In this kind of intensive gardening legumes must never, under any circumstances, be lacking!

Early in March, 1939, the same land was thoroughly worked and the ridges and troughs exchanged. Preparation 500 was sprayed three times, before the early Spring planting, before planting in late Spring and before the last planting in late Summer. Prepared compost or manure-earth was put in the plant holes or seed furrows at planting time. Preparation 501 was applied repeatedly in the course of the growing season. (Not, however, to germinating seeds or plants ripe for harvest.) All these preparations come to complete effectiveness when used on mixed cultures. The arrangement in ridges considerably increases the area available and makes it possible to have smaller spaces between the plants because of the different levels on which they are grown.

Planting Plan, 1939

	Crests	Sides	Troughs
Spring:	Spinach & Kohl-rabi	Radishes	Kohl-rabi & Lettuce
	Lettuce & Kohl-rabi	Early & Late Carrots	
		Leaf Lettuce & Radishes	
Summer & Fall:	Celeriac & Lettuce	Late sowing of Early Carrots Lettuce, Celeriac, Radishes, Endive	Bush Beans Beets & Leeks

Bordering the length of the garden, both sides: Peas, Late Endive.
On the vertical ends of the ridges: Garden Cress.

Root vegetables, when grown in the troughs, do not develop very large roots in comparison to their leaf mass (too much shade).

Leaf vegetables develop well everywhere.
The following were harvested from the area in 1939:

Spinach	3.858 lbs.	String Beans	11.463	lbs.
Garden Cress	3.527 "	Leeks	9.920	"
Late Carrots	30.577 "	Celeriac leaves	5.511	"
Celeriac	14.991 "	Lettuce	61	heads
Beets	26.455 "	Endive	51	"
Leaf Lettuce	6.613 "	Kohl-rabi (1 lb. ea.)	41	pieces
Early Carrots	21.164 "	Radishes	550	"

Such high yields are made possible by the fine, symmetrical development of plants grown in this manner, and by the above-mentioned beneficial effect of the bio-dynamic preparations.

This concentration of production on a small area requires a corresponding concentration of labor. The following statement gives a detailed picture of this. The notes are taken from the diary of a home gardener.

Labor	*Month*	*Hours*	
Preparatory labor of laying out the ridges and bringing compost	Mid-April	8	
Sowing, planting & thinning: Kohl-rabi, head lettuce, summer radishes, chard, leaf lettuce, peas, carrots, garden cress		2	
Sowing, replanting, harvesting: Bush beans, kohl-rabi, lettuce, garden cress		1	10 min.
Weeding and hoeing, manuring	End of May	6	
Harvesting: Leaf lettuce, kohl-rabi, radishes, chard, head lettuce, peas	End of May		
Hoeing and watering	June	2	15 min.
Hoeing and watering	June		30 min.
Harvesting: Kohl-rabi, chard, radishes, peas	July		40 min.
Sowing: Late turnips, bush beans	August		
Thinning, planting: Carrots, leeks, endive	August		

68

Harvesting: Early carrots, peas, kohl-
rabi, bush beans, beets, beans, chard,
late carrots...................... 4   50 min.
Hoeing and weeding................ August 2

27 hr. 25 min.

The following table gives the yield of another garden of this
type from the 11th of May to the 10th of August:

Yield in Pounds

Cress......................	2
Spinach....................	16
Chard.....................	11½
Early radishes..............	4
Carrots....................	2
Beans.....................	5
Onions....................	5
Summer radishes............	14½
Head lettuce...............	33
Kohl-rabi..................	15½
Cabbage...................	22
Total yield.........130½ lbs.	

There are still some details to be reported from the practical
experiences of 1940. In a very sunny location it makes quite a
difference in which direction the ridges are set up, whether they
run from east to west or from north to south. Carrots, for example, grew much better on the eastern slopes and more quickly,
too, than on the western slopes. Radishes suffered less from flea
beetles when they were grown on the eastern slopes. On the contrary, bush beans grew better on ridges which ran to the west. We
can compensate for such differences by maintaining a careful
ground cover. This enables us to obtain that quick growth *in the
very beginning,* which later forms the special advantage of the
ridge type garden plan.

69

6. Practical Cultural Directions for the Various Vegetables

THE CABBAGE FAMILY IN GENERAL

SOIL and fertilizer requirements. The members of the cabbage family are all heavy consumers of humus, require water and all nutritive substances in order to form their great leaf masses in the course of the growing season. All types of cabbage belong in the "first rank." They love a rich, black humus. Cauliflower requires, in addition, a warm soil and a warm location. Some lime content in the soil is necessary to all cabbage sorts. Cauliflower is frequently planted on freshly broken soil, but a good garden soil is preferable, if a proper crop rotation has been conscientiously followed in its previous cultivation.

Crop rotation. In the small garden it is important to follow a regulated crop rotation when growing cabbages, although this is sometimes difficult. If cabbage is often followed by cabbage, the inevitable result is club-root and all such diseases, as well as the cabbage butterfly, cabbage worm, and other pests. Club-root, the most dangerous of all the distorting diseases, is the immediate result of not rotating the crops. It can also be introduced by infected seedlings. The single, sure remedy against it is the elimination of cabbage culture (and of all the Crucifers) for four or five years. The soil can also be disinfected with heavy applications of lime. These are not good, however, unless preceded by humus fertilizing. Cabbage stalks should always be burned and their ashes put on the compost heap. The leaves can be composted if they are not needed for cattle fodder. It has been observed that leeks grown before and after cabbage, on beds infected with club-root, have a healthful influence.

Growing plants. The seeds are sown in a coldframe or seed bed and are transplanted once, at which time they should be set deeper. Seedlings to be wintered over are sown in August, transplanted in September, and set out in four inch furrows in October. In less favorable years, they are set out the following March or April.

Freshly planted cabbage, having not yet developed its deeper roots, needs lots of moisture in order to make a sure growth. It is expedient to dip the root balls in a paste made of clay and preparation 500 at the time of setting out. If we do this, we can completely eliminate watering, if we are planting on an overcast day. (Cloudy weather is real planting weather anyhow.) Do not transplant in the blazing sun! Refined compost can be put in the planting furrow or plant hole.

Cultivation. All cabbage sorts must be regularly and thoroughly hoed. In a light soil, high hilling is indispensable, in order to hold the moisture around their roots. This is also customary in every other type of soil. We should be careful to keep the ground covered, at first, by interplantings of lettuce, early kohlrabi, or bush beans. Later, the mature plants themselves provide the best ground cover.

The growing plant is very grateful for an application of well-rotted manure. It is easier to do this in the small garden, of course, than in the case of field culture. If there is no manure available, it helps, especially in dry weather, at least, to put a ring of straw, hay, shavings, or half-rotted leaves around the plants. Oak leaves and oak bark, which are hostile to pests, are excellent material for such a mulch.

Harvesting. Early cabbage is harvested as soon as it is ripe enough for use. Late cabbage, to be stored over Winter, is harvested as late as possible, up to the end of November. The most sensitive to frost is red cabbage. The hardiest is savoy cabbage, which can stand temperatures 12 degrees below freezing without spoiling.

Storing. The best place to store cabbage is an empty coldframe which is dry and free of frost, and can be ventilated. The heads, with the roots still attached, are plunged in sand. Another method which is good is to bury them in open ground in a protected place where the temperature will be fairly even (on the north wall of a stable, for example). The heads are placed with the roots upward and lightly covered with earth. When severe weather sets in a light rush or straw cover should be added.

Cabbage must be carefully, but not too thoroughly, trimmed before it is stored. Over-ripe, burst, or undeveloped heads should not be stored. On convenient days the buried cabbage is checked over and rotting heads removed.

Seed growing. All types of cabbage cross with one another. If it is not possible to grow different varieties at great distances from one another then *one* kind only is grown for seed.

The firmest heads are selected and stored very carefully over Winter. These are set out early in the following April. They must be set quite deeply and support provided for the seed stalks. The seed must be protected from the birds. (Grape gauze.) The mature seed stalks are hung indoors and allowed to dry until it is possible to thresh them or remove the seed by hand.

CABBAGE VARIETIES

White and Red Cabbage, Savoy Cabbage.

We present only certain proved varieties, since we are not in a position to consider the numerous local variants. A consideration of all possible varieties would overstep the bounds of this small book.

Proven varieties: White cabbage, early: Golden Acre, Charleston or Early Jersey Wakefield. White cabbage, late: Danish Ball-head, Copenhagen Market, Wisconsin Hollander. Red cabbage, early: Danish Round Red. Late: Mammoth Red Rock. Savoy, early: Cornell Early Savoy. Late: Perfection Drumhead. For wintering over: Succession.

Early varieties. These are sown in the hotbed in February/ March. They are transplanted once and set out in the garden in April/May.

For wintering over. Sow in August, transplant once. Set out in October or March/April.

Planting distances for early varieties: 1 by 2 feet.

Late varieties. Sow in March/April in coldframes or seed beds.

If transplanted seedlings have to be held over longer than usual and seem to be cramped for light, water and nourishment, they should be transplanted for a second time. Nothing is worse than stunted plants, especially in a dry soil. They die off easily, while sturdy seedlings can still hold out. Too thickly sown or transplanted seedlings are apt to develop black leg. Cauliflower is especially susceptible to this.

Late varieties are set out in May/June.

Harvest: of the wintered over sorts: June, July.

of early varieties: July to September.

of late varieties: October, November.

Planting distances for late varieties: 2 by 2½ feet.

Culture. Early savoy cabbage is particularly suited to use as a border planting for cucumber beds or it can be set out in alternate rows with late cabbage to make use of the space. Early red cabbage can also be alternated with late cabbage in the same way. Those working bio-dynamically, spray preparation 501 when the plants are well along in growth and the first indications of heading are apparent.

KOHL-RABI

Early varieties: White Vienna, Earliest Erfurt.

Sowing: February/March in a coldframe, transplant once.

Setting out: After the days of the Ice Saints.[1]
In April and May sow in the open; transplant once.
Setting out: May, June and again in August. (Correspondingly later sowing in the garden, one transplanting.)
Late varieties: Purple Vienna, Green Vienna. Sow in seed bed in April and May, transplant once.
Setting out: June, for Fall harvest.
Planting distances: according to variety and soil, 6 to 8 inches.
Cultivation and care. Kohl-rabi must be hoed and watered diligently so that it remains tender and does not get leggy. It can be grown successfully in a light soil if it is watered sufficiently and receives enough compost. Preparation 500 is applied at the time of setting out. 501 is given after the plants are established and begin to form bulbs.
Harvesting. The bulb, which grows above ground, is a very delicious vegetable if used before it gets tough. It should be picked when it is about 2 inches across, not more.
Place in the rotation. Kohl-rabi is very useful as a precrop and intercrop, especially the small early varieties, White Vienna, for instance. It does well between late cabbage or cauliflower, or in alternation with savoy cabbage or celeriac on the edges of cucumber beds. It is also good between lettuce.

CAULIFLOWER

Varieties: Dwarf Erfurt. This is the most expensive but the most reliable early variety. Early Snowball is also good. Late cauliflower needs so much space, warmth and fertilizing that it scarcely comes into consideration for the home garden. However, a usable variety is Veitch's Autumn Giant.
Sowing. Cauliflower is sown very carefully in a hotbed in February or March. It should be transplanted twice.

---

[1] These are the days of Pancracius, Servacius, Bonifacius, and Sophia and fall on the 12th, 13th, 14th and 15th of May, respectively.

In general it is better to purchase seedlings from a reliable gardener. Set out only well hardened seedlings!

Care. Cauliflower land should receive an application of prepared manure in the Fall. This is then spaded in and the area is left lying over winter in rough clods. Preparation 500 is applied in the Fall and in the Spring. Quite ripe, good, earthy compost can be put in the planting holes, or better still be used as a mulch. Cauliflower must be watered without fail in dry weather. If the leaves do not grow high enough to blanch the developing heads (the single disadvantage of Dwarf Erfurt!) it helps to tie them together.

CURLED OR WINTER KALE

Low curled varieties, Dwarf Green Curled and Dwarf Blue Scotch, for example, are preferable to the tall growing varieties, particularly in regions of frequent snows and thaws, alternating with severe periods of frost.

Sowing. It is sown in the garden beds from the middle of May to the end of June. Kale is usually sown thus in the open and thinned rather than transplanted.

Distances. Thin to greater distances in heavy soils to prevent rotting of the lower leaves. Usual distances are 8 to 15 inches apart in the row.

BRUSSELS SPROUTS

Varieties: Long Island Improved, Long Island Half Dwarf, Danish Prize and Paris White.

Sowing. Sow in May in seed bed, transplant once.

Setting out. Set seedlings out in June/July.

Planting distances. 1 to 2 feet apart in the rows, 2 to 2½ feet between the rows.

Both kale and brussels sprouts when succeeding peas or early potatoes, receive preparation 500 in the planting holes and some prepared compost or composted manure as a mulch. From our own observation brussels sprouts can well be planted after chamomile which has been grown for the blossoms. If brussels sprouts do not form solid sprouts the plants may be topped in September or October. However, this should not be done too early. Since these tops and the loose rosettes can be cooked and used as a green, topping is often practiced when living costs are high.

Harvesting. This begins after the sprouts are formed. When severe frost sets in, the whole stalks can be pulled out and stored in earth in the cellar. Kale can stay out over winter.

Harvest the larger leaves of kale and preserve the hearts.

Both kale and brussels sprouts are greatly improved in flavor by light frost.

HEAD LETTUCE

Varieties: 1. Early: May King.

2. Early Summer: Big Boston, Imperial No. 44.

3. Summer: Stuttgart Wonder, Iceberg.

4. For wintering over: Wayahead.

Sowing. 1. Sow in flats and forcing beds in January/February, transplant once or twice. Set out in coldframes in March/April, in April in the open. Lettuce sowings should be repeated every two or three weeks.

2. & 3. Sow at the end of March, repeat up to end of May, corresponding transplanting and setting out.

4. Sow in August and September. Set out in 5 inch furrows in September and October. Give light protective covering of some sort.

We feel fortunate indeed when we can have home grown lettuce in the Winter!

Soil and cultivation requirements. Head lettuce is a true garden plant and favors a warm, humus soil. It becomes leggy and does not head well in a raw, heavy soil. It forms the finest heads in a soil which has long been under cultivation, if it is hoed carefully and watered daily during dry periods.

It follows, therefore, that it is particularly suited to culture in hotbeds or under movable coldframes. Careful ventilation is necessary.

Preparation 500 is applied before sowing or planting. When the plants begin to form little whorls spray 501 and repeat this if they tend to bolt to seed.

Seed growing. Select two or three of the firmest heads, from amongst those which are slowest to bolt to seed, and leave them in the garden to blossom. The large inflorescence should be well staked. When a large portion of the seeds is already developed pull the plants out and hang them in the shade to dry.

All the members of the finch family eagerly lie in wait for lettuce seeds. The removing and cleaning of the seeds is a rather tedious task which can be done in the Winter.

LOOSE-LEAF LETTUCE

Varieties: Black-seeded Simpson.
Grand Rapids: especially good for forcing.

Sowing. The advantages of the loose-leaf over the heading varieties are in their quicker growth and greater resistance to heat. Therefore early Spring sowings at the same time as is recommended for head lettuce will provide edible leaves sooner. Sow small amounts of seed at repeated intervals. It can be thinned and used gradually, beginning while the leaves are still quite small. It can also be sown later in the Spring than head lettuce, which bolts to seed more quickly in hot weather.

Culture. In general this is the same as for head lettuce except that transplanting is usually not worth while because of its quick growth. It is also somewhat less particular as to soil requirements.

77

Varieties: Escarolle, Giant Fringed Oyster; Deep Heart, or Improved Full Heart. Endive is a good substitute for head lettuce during the Fall and Winter.

Sowing. For harvest in August, sow in April in a cold-frame. For harvest in October, sow in the open, June 15th-30th. Transplant or thin.

Planting distances. Three rows to a bed, 12 to 18 inches apart in the rows.

Soil and fertilizing. Endive needs more warmth than head lettuce and likes a rich, well-manured soil. As a rule we manure the preceding crop and spray preparation 500 before setting out or sowing the endive. It is preferable, however, to give endive a mulch of half-rotted manure compost.

Care. When setting out, prune the roots and tops of the plants slightly. The moisture needs of the young plants are great. Nearly mature plants are tied with raffia to blanch them. Tying should be done only when the plants are dry. It is important, however, not to blanch more plants than can be used up at one time. The blanched heads are usable within two weeks after they are tied.

Harvesting and storing. Before severe frosts set in, the plants are dug with a good-sized ball of earth and buried in an empty coldframe or stored in the cellar in sand. The heads blanch in the dark without being tied. The danger of rotting is always great so that, as a rule, endive cannot be wintered over in the garden. Curled or fringed endive is more sensitive to frost, more tender than the broadleaved varieties.

Seed culture does not come into question for the small gardener.

CORN SALAD OR LAMB'S LETTUCE

Varieties: Large-leaved Round.

Sowing. Corn salad can be sown from the end of August to the beginning of September in every cleared and criled garden bed.

It is usually sown broadcast. In very weedy land, however, it should be sown in rows, six to a bed, so that it can be hoed. Firm the seeds down well. In the small garden it can be watered in dry weather.

The fertilizer given to the preceding crop is sufficient for this vegetable. It is good to spray 500 before sowing.

Harvesting. Corn salad can be harvested all through the Winter, in open weather, on into the Spring. It quickly bolts to seed in May as soon as the weather becomes dry and warm.

Seeds can be gathered in June from wintered over plants. They should not be allowed to get too ripe, however, as they fall out very easily.

SPINACH

Varieties: Bloomsdale Longstanding, Nobel (both Winter hardy), Old Dominion, Giant Smooth Leaf dark green, and countless others.

Sowing. Sow in February/March for early Summer harvest, end of July, beginning of August for Fall harvest. The main sowing takes place at the end of August or beginning of September to stand over Winter. This sowing is harvested in April and May.

Sow six rows in each bed and mark them with radishes. Only Spring seedings are sown broadcast. April sowings are apt to bolt to seed.

Sow in shallow furrows, cover carefully with compost, firm down well. Carefully covered seeds are saved from the birds.

Soil and fertilizer requirements. Spinach likes a soil which is rich in humus, but not too heavy. It never does well in an acid soil. Good fertilizing with prepared manure compost is necessary. In dry weather spinach requires diligent watering. Prepared liquid manure may be applied after cutting, never fresh liquid manure. The application of preparation 500 before sowing is especially useful as in the case of all humus loving plants. The

79

correct application of 501 (after the young leaves have completely unfolded) hinders bolting to seed.

Cultivation. Weeds must be kept down by using a scuffle hoe or a similar shallow weeder. Should the spinach threaten to bolt to seed a second spraying of 501 often helps.

CHARD

Varieties: Fordhook Giant, Large Ribbed White.

Sowing. Sow in April; five to six rows of Fordhook Giant, two to three rows of Large Ribbed White. Too thickly sown chard of the latter variety is used like spinach. The final distance in the row, after thinning, should be 12 inches. The ribbed type of chard may be sown in succession, with beets or lettuce as a companion crop, or seedlings may be set out.

Cultivation. It should constantly be kept thoroughly hoed and weeded. It is grateful for watering.

Fertilizer. Chard loves "turnip soil," that is a heavy, humus, loamy soil and consumes poorer soils. Applications of fresh, liquid manure and fresh manure make it bitter and earthy in flavor. The stems get spotty and very tough. It is best, then, to fertilize chard with prepared mixed compost or rotted stable manure and water it with prepared liquid manure after cutting. Preparation 500, applied before sowing or planting, and 501, applied after the formation of the young leaves, promote a healthy leaf growth and a fine aroma.

Harvesting. Neither the leaves nor the stems should be cut too deeply. In the rib type, the heart leaves must be left undisturbed.

CUCUMBERS

Varieties: Straight Eight and Black Diamond. For pickling purposes, Fordhook Pickling, Jersey Pickle and Everbearing.

Sowing. Sow in pots (paper pots are good) or hotbeds from the middle to the end of April. They are sown in the open after the days of the Ice Saints are past. In warm localities or in warm years they can be sown shortly before this. Cucumbers should be sown in a *warm* soil.

Soil, fertilizer, and cultivation requirements. Cucumbers like a warm, not too heavy, muck soil, rich in humus and nutritive substances. In other words, "black" soils meet the needs of the cucumber. Without doubt, it belongs in the "first rank." In the garden it is best to plant cucumbers on long hills or ridges of manure compost. Sods or quack grass composted with horse manure yield the most superior cucumber earth. Ridges of such compost are built up through the middle of the normal garden bed, leaving a ten inch border free. The garden earth is then lightly pulled up over this ridge and the seeds are pressed in along the crest five or six inches apart. Later, the plants should be thinned to stand one to two feet apart.

Setting out. The seedlings can be set out after the middle of May, in a warm soil. Care should be taken to keep a good earth ball on the roots. The planting distance is again about two feet. During the first days they should be shaded, up-turned flower pots are handy for this. Watering should be done with lukewarm water.

Pruning. After the appearance of the third to the fifth leaf, the tips of the vines may be pinched back so that they will branch.

Watering. Cucumbers need an abundance of water. Thorough watering twice a week is better than daily superficial watering. Always use water which has *stood in the air and sun,* never spray cucumbers with a hose!

Companion and border plantings. The hills can easily support one sowing of radishes. The borders can carry companion plantings of kohl-rabi and lettuce, kohl-rabi and early savoy cabbage, celeriac and lettuce or bush beans, or lettuce and radishes. Cucumbers like some sort of light protection. They thrive well in alternation with rows of sweet corn. The cucumber rows should

81

then be at least six and a half feet apart. Canning factories often plant them in alternation with early potatoes and early cabbage, with wide spacing. This is also a good combination.

Seed growing. We can always have our own cucumber seed if we let the earliest maturing, fine, well formed, healthy fruits from healthy plants, hang until ripe. The seeds are scraped out of the fully ripe cucumbers. They are then put in a warm place in a little water to ferment. Afterward, put them in a sieve and wash them, dry them gently with a cloth and then spread them out on blotting paper until they are completely dry.

SUMMER AND WINTER SQUASH

Varieties: Zucchini Bush, Cocozelle Bush, Mammoth White Bush, Golden Summer Crookneck, Acorn, True Hubbard, Blue Hubbard.

Sowing. Sow in pots the middle of April, in the open after May 20th.

The great greediness of squash can be satisfied by planting it at the *foot* of manure or compost heaps. There it makes use of excess moisture and washed out nutritive substances besides climbing over the heap and shading it with its tendrils. Prepared liquid manure aids its growth. If the fruit sets too thickly it should be thinned out. Soil, warmth, fertilizer and water requirements are even greater than those of the cucumber.

Seed is grown in the same way as was described for cucumbers.

SWEET CORN

Varieties: Golden Bantam, Marcross, Whipple's Early Yellow, Golden Cross Bantam, Golden Colonel. (These are all yellow-seeded varieties which have become very popular in recent years. Two good, tried and true white varieties are Country Gentleman and Stowell's Evergreen. A good early white variety is Span-cross.)

Sowing. Sow in the open after the first of May.

Culture and care. Make deep furrows or plant holes in good rich soil which has lain over Winter in rough clods. These holes or furrows are then sprayed with preparation 500. Fill them with prepared manure and cover this lightly with earth. Sow every three to four inches in the furrows and thin later to ten inches. In the hills, sow four or five grains and thin to two or three stalks, at most. Distance between the rows or between the hills two and a half to three feet. In the small garden, corn is suitable for an annual border planting on the south or west sides. Hoe diligently and hill high. Watering can then be omitted. In drought years a mulch of half-ripe manure compost is good.

Harvesting. The ears are ripe enough when the silk at the tips has turned dark brown. If we want corn to ripen more quickly we can remove the tassels as soon as all the pollen has disappeared. (Before this, they are necessary for fructification.)

Seed growing. The earliest, best-developed, full-grained ears are allowed to ripen on the stalk. (Hybrid varieties do not produce fertile seed.) When the husks are bleached and straw-like, pick the ears, pull the husks back, tie two ears together and hang them up to dry.

Companion plants. Corn is a great soil consumer and often leaves an exhausted soil behind. We like, therefore, to plant it in company with bush beans or soya beans, which shade the soil, make it friable and have a generally favorable influence upon it. We have already spoken about companion cropping with cucumbers.

CELERIAC

Varieties: Giant Prague.

Sowing. In the small garden sowing in the open is not advisable. The very fine seeds are sown in a hotbed the middle of February. They should be transplanted twice.

Setting out. The seedlings are set out in May/June. Distance between the rows, one and a half to two feet, distance in the

83

row, ten to twelve inches, according to the soil and the variety.

Soil and culture requirements. Celeriac flourishes in a black, muck soil; that is, a soil rich in humus or a garden soil which has been long under cultivation. It is often grown successfully in newly broken ground but this is connected with the fact that it is extremely sensitive to itself. It should be planted again on the same spot only after four years. As a potassium consumer celeriac is thankful for well-rotted, earthy, pig manure.

Care. Hoe carefully to work against crusting of the soil, but do not hill. Celeriac develops better knobs if it is not hilled. Water thoroughly, also with prepared liquid manure or prepared manure water. Fresh liquid manure applications are very harmful, causing rust and black rot. Preparation 500 is applied before planting and 501 after the seedlings are well established. Both of these sprays are particularly important in the case of celeriac. Repeated sprayings of horse-tail tea (Equisetum arvense) help against the formation of rust.

Harvesting. Celeriac is harvested in November, as late as possible. It continues to make some growth up to the beginning of Winter. Cut the leaves back to the heart and bury the knobs in the cool and frost proof root pit.

Seed growing. This does not come into consideration for the small gardener.

Companion plants. Celeriac likes to have air and space and grows well in a light stand in alternate rows with leeks or bush beans. Head lettuce can also serve as a companion crop. It is more neutral, however, while leeks and bush beans are actively beneficial.

LEEKS

Varieties: This mild-flavored member of the onion family produces no bulb but is relished for its enlarged stem, much like a Spring onion. It may be used raw in salads or cooked like onions.

84

The varieties best known are Large American Flag and Elephant.

Sowing. Leeks are sown in flats or coldframes in February/ March. They must always be transplanted.

Soil and fertilizer requirements. A very loamy, not too clayey soil rich in humus suits leeks best. Prepared manure is spread in the Fall, ploughed or spaded in and the area is left lying over Winter in rough clods. (The addition of a certain amount of pig manure is excellent.) Leeks do well after potatoes. Watering is not necessary. Applications of prepared manure water or pre-pared liquid manure are stimulating. However, we must be care-ful not to over-force leeks with fertilizer. They will then become thick and massive, of course, but will have a harsh flavor.

Culture. Set out in April/May. Distance between the rows not less than a foot, wide enough to make furrows six inches deep. The furrows are sprayed with preparation 500. Trim the tops and roots of the seedlings slightly and set them as deeply as possible. The first hoeings will fill up the furrows. Later the leeks should be hilled repeatedly until the hills are about as high as the fur-rows were deep.

Harvesting. Leeks are harvested in November unless we intend to winter them over in the open. Store them in a trench until May or June of the coming year. The leeks which have been left in the garden over Winter are taken up in the Spring to prevent their blossoming and are also put in the storage pit or trench. Blanching them in the ground through high hilling is preferable to blanching them after they have been taken up.

Seed bearers are hilled very high to protect them from freezing in the Winter. The plants should stand at least a foot and a half apart in all directions. The blossom stem needs good support. Leeks cross easily with pearl onions. The seeds mature fully only in favorable Summers and in a warm situation.

Companion plants. Leeks are good neighbors with celeriac, bush beans and beets.

Varieties: (Seed and onion sets.) Yellow Globe Danvers, Southport White Globe, White Portugal. Japanese Long Bunching (can be wintered over). White Multiplier Sets, Yellow Sets.

Sowing. 1. For the Winter supply sow in February in the hotbed, transplant once perhaps, later set out in the open, or sow in the open in March.

2. For wintering over and use in the early Summer sow in the open from June to July.

3. For growing onion sets, sow thickly in a light, warm soil, from April to June.

4. Onion sets are planted in the open at the end of March. "St. Benedict (March 21st) makes onions thick."

In cases 1, 2, and 4 make six rows per bed. Thin out plants where they have germinated too thickly and use them to fill out gaps in the rows. The final distance in the row should be four to five inches.

When growing onion sets, sow eight rows in each bed or sow broadcast in weed free land. Sow the seed as thinly as possible in shallow furrows, firm down very well. (This is best done with a board or the back of a spade.)

Onion sets, when planted, are pressed down firmly in shallow furrows, in any case firm the soil well over them. The sets should be pushed down to a depth of an inch or an inch and a half.

Cultivation. Onions must be kept very free of weeds and well cultivated. In the first stages of their growth loosen the soil shallowly. Even later do not hoe deeply. The evaporation of the soil moisture is checked by such skillful hoeing. Onions cannot stand being watered.

Soil and fertilizer requirements. Warm, fairly dry, not too heavy soils, long under cultivation, are favored by onions. The concept "onion soil" can scarcely be fully defined. The ground

86

should be rough spaded in the Fall so that it can be sown as soon as possible in Spring. Members of the cabbage family, cucumbers and celeriac are suitable pre-crops. June and July sowings may be preceded by early potatoes and peas. Chamomile, also, forms a beneficial predecessor for onions. In a sandy soil, where onions ordinarily do not like to grow, they can be brought to a happier growth by having a few chamomile plants standing in the same bed. Since onions cannot endure any kind of fresh fertilizer, the use of preparation 500 is exceedingly important. Do not apply preparation 501 too soon, the little bulbs should be formed already.

Harvesting. Onions are harvested as soon as the tops have wilted and dried up. In wet seasons, this process can be speeded up by trampling the tops. Harvest them in dry weather. They should then be spread out in an airy place to dry out well or cure.

On small places they are sometimes tied together in bunches and hung up to dry.

Seed growing. Select solid, well-ripened onions, which were grown from sets the previous year. These should be set out as early in the year as possible in sunny, wind-protected situations. The blossom stems must be carefully supported. A mulch of manure compost is good. The seeds ripen slowly and must be dried under cover. (They fall out easily!) Ripe seeds are coal black.

GARLIC

Cultivated from the most ancient times and often scorned because of its strong flavor, garlic can nevertheless be a very useful herb in the hands of an expert cook. A small amount is easily grown in the home garden by dividing the bulb and planting the individual "cloves" about two inches deep and four inches apart in the row. These can be set out early with the onion sets, harvested in Midsummer when the leaves turn yellow, and dried in the sun for several days.

SHALLOTS

These are small members of the onion family which deserve more common use since they are milder flavored than onions and much more easily cultivated, only needing to have the weeds kept down during the growing season. The hollow leaves are also used in their green state for flavoring. The bulbs are grown from the separated "cloves" in the same way as garlic, except that each clove is set barely under the surface of the soil. They should be set ten inches apart since they multiply during growth. They are easily separated at the base when harvested. Lift the group when the stalks turn yellow and, like garlic, hang up to dry for several days before storing. They keep well if stored like onions in a moderately cool, dry and airy place.

CARROTS

Varieties: A distinction is generally made between the first early carrots, which can also be grown under glass, and the medium early and late varieties, which are grown in the open.

Forcing varieties: Early Golden Ball and Amsterdam Forcing, Very Early Short Horn or French Forcing. Their yield is small and they require a real humus, garden soil long in culture.

Later varieties: Nantes Half-Long and Touchon. (Both coreless.) Chantenay Half-Long and Danvers Half-Long. These like a more loamy soil.

Sowing. Carrots are sown as soon as the ground is open. Main sowings are made in March and April. For winter use sow in the middle of May. Repeated sowings of the earlier varieties can be made, as needed, up to the beginning of July. Choose well-cleaned seed, mark the rows with a very light sowing of lettuce, spinach, or radishes.

Sow five or six rows of early carrots, four or five of later varieties, per bed. Never broadcast carrot seed. Make furrows two inches deep, spray them lightly with preparation 500, and put prepared compost in them. After sowing, these furrows are drawn lightly together and the seed is firmed down with the back of the rake. In the case of Summer sowings it is particularly good to cover the whole bed lightly with compost.

Summer care. Regular weeding and shallow cultivating or hoeing are necessary for carrots. Too thickly grown seedings should be thinned. Water only while the plants are still small. After thinning they can be given prepared manure water. If they are attacked by root lice a mulch of composted oak leaves and oak bark, which are rich in tannin, is helpful.

Harvesting. Carrot harvesting is continual, since the strongest roots are constantly being pulled for use. Before they are in danger of splitting or becoming maggoty, they should all be pulled. This should be done when the soil is not too dry in order to avoid breaking them.

Storing. Cut the tops back, but not too short, do not injure the crowns. Store the healthy, dry carrots in sand in the cellar or in an empty coldframe without any inner layering.

Seed growing. Carefully keep the best developed roots with medium tops, over Winter. Set these out in March, twelve to twenty inches apart, according to the variety. The cultural requirements are the same as those given under Summer care. Seed stock must not be forced! Cut the ripe umbels, dry them in the shade, rub the chaff out by hand. Seed propagation only has sense if the area is not surrounded with meadow land, since the wild carrot (Queen Anne's Lace) crosses with the garden carrot.

Companion plants. Carrots are compatible with soil loosening plants. Best known is their friendship with peas. Flax ought to be experimented with as a companion crop in field culture. Occasional rows of flax scattered through a field, loosen even the toughest soil to an uncommon degree.

Varieties: The oval and turnip shaped types are better liked for household use than the long conical sorts. The Flat Egyptian is an old proven variety. Eclipse, Crosby Early Wonder and Detroit Dark Red are also good.

Sowing. Beets are sown in succession from April to June. June sowings yield beets for use in the Winter until after the New Year. Later sowings are not likely to mature.

Sow the large seeds quite thinly, four rows per bed. Preparation 500 is applied before sowing. If the soil is too light, dry, or tough, mulch it lightly with compost. Diligent watering furthers germination.

If the seeds germinate poorly in spots these can be filled out with young plants from more thickly germinated parts of the rows. The beets should be three to four inches apart in the rows. Transplant only on cloudy days as beets wilt easily.

Cultivation and fertilizer. Beets should be diligently cultivated and hoed. Keep the soil from crusting until the leaves are large enough to shade it. Liquid manure is not necessary in a cultivated, not too light soil. Too much of it impairs the flavor and keeping quality of beets. Preparation 501 is applied shortly before the first or second picking.

Harvesting. The beets ready for use are pulled as needed until the correct distance in the row is reached. Finally the whole bed is cleared.

Storing. Beets are stored, frost free, in sand. The tops should be cut quite short, but care should be taken not to injure the roots. Seed beets should be kept over Winter in coldframes without the layers of sand. A covering of nut leaves is a protection against mice.

Seed growing. The perfectly formed beets, which have been kept over Winter, are set out early in April about twenty inches apart. The ripe seed stalks are cut and hung in the shade to dry. Later, the seeds are rubbed out by hand.

Companion plants. Beets, when grown in a heavy soil, like the company of bush beans and soya beans. They also grow well in alternation with beds of leeks and rows of kohl-rabi.

RADISHES

Varieties: For forcing and early harvest in the open, Early Scarlet Globe and French Breakfast. White Icicle and Early Long Scarlet mature somewhat later.

Summer radishes: Chartiers (rosy red), White Strassburg.

Winter radishes: White Chinese, Long Black Spanish, Japanese Colossal.

Sowing. Early radishes are sown in hotbeds, from the beginning of February; under movable coldframes in March; in the open, from the beginning of April. Sowings can be repeated every two weeks until the middle or end of May.

Summer radishes are sown every three or four weeks from the middle of April to the beginning of June.

Winter radishes are sown in June for a late harvest.

Radishes should be sown very thinly. Too thick sowings must be thinned.

Soil and cultivation requirements. In order to be tender, early radishes need a warm, humus soil (prepared compost or hotbed earth), abundant moisture and a mild temperature. In rough or dry soil, with heavy fertilizing or great heat, they become coarse, strawy, woody, and fuzzy.

Summer and winter radishes also thrive well in heavy, loamy soils, if these have been long under cultivation. Even good, prepared compost does not compensate for long years of cultivation.

Raw soils and strong fertilizing (fresh liquid manure) make radishes wormy. They do not belong in the "first rank." Preparation 500 and prepared compost are particularly effective in the development of tender, aromatic radishes.

The flea beetle is the deadly enemy of all radishes. It is less likely to appear if the soil is kept cultivated, mulched, and shaded. If it is once present, the soil should be watered repeatedly in the full sun. Ordinarily, of course, we rightly avoid watering in the blazing sun.

Place in the rotation. Radishes are ideal for intercropping. Early radishes may be sown in the hotbed between rows of forcing carrots, early seedlings, lettuce, spinach, and in the furrows with spinach and carrots to mark the rows.

They may also be sown on the borders of cucumber beds, as companion plants for early kohl-rabi and in seed beds.

Summer and winter radishes do well in alternation with bush beans and beets or pole beans.

Harvesting. Radishes are pulled as they mature and are ready for use.

Seed growing. Seed culture occasionally succeeds with early radishes. The plants which bolt to seed *quite late* are left standing. The blossoming plants are very brittle and must be carefully staked. The harvested seed stalks ripen completely when hung in the shade. It is difficult to protect them from the finches.

EARLY TURNIPS AND RUTABAGAS

Varieties: Purple-Top White Globe, Early Red and many others. It is not advisable to sow the early types in the garden as they easily fall prey to flea beetles.

Fall turnips or rutabagas make an excellent after crop since they can still be sown in July. A good variety is the Long Island Neckless Purple Top Rutabaga.

The Japanese Foliage Turnip is an excellent variety grown for its leafy top, though the white roots may also be used. It is treated like other turnips. Early Spring sowings seem to produce the best results.

Sowing. Rutabagas are sown in freshly criled land which has previously been fertilized with compost. They may be sown broadcast, but better in rows a foot to a foot and a half apart. Preparation 500 is applied before sowing as is usual with new plantings during the season. In dry weather, watering helps to hold the flea beetles in check. 501 is no longer applied due to the lateness of the season. Hoe when necessary. Thin to four or five inches in the row.

Place in the rotation. Rutabagas should not succeed cabbage, because of their close relationship. We have found from experience that they are healing to soils which have become hard and crusted through extreme fluctuations in temperature and storms. Their effect is also excellent after early potatoes which had had to be harvested during wet weather.

Harvesting. They are harvested in October or November and kept over Winter in the same way as beets.

Seed growing. The chosen plants are lightly covered and remain in the ground over Winter. In the Spring they should be uncovered early. Further treatment is the same ·as in the case of beets.

FENNEL OR FINOCCHIO

Varieties: Florence Fennel.

Sowing. Finocchio can be sown from the 25th of June to the 10th of July. It is a good idea to make two sowings, since sometimes the earlier, sometimes the later sowing succeeds better. Sow fairly thickly, three rows per bed, later thin to three or four inches. The beds should be mounded slightly to further drainage. Sow in shallow furrows in good compost earth.

Soil, planting and cultural requirements. Fennel likes a warm location and a good garden soil. It belongs in the "second rank." However, it should not succeed cabbage since its nutritive demands are quite high. It does better after early potatoes or early peas. When planted after peas it should receive an abundance of compost. It is grateful for preparation 500.

It tends to bolt to seed and must, therefore, be watered thoroughly and often in dry times. It should be hoed frequently and kept free of weeds. Hill up with earth to blanch the knob-like leaf base.

Harvesting. Fennel is harvested in the Fall. Early frosts may be injurious hence the July sowing must not be put off too long. May sowings are apt to go to seed before the knobs have developed.

Seed growing. Fennel is ordinarily a perennial plant which can remain in one place for three or four years. We recommend the annual type because it gives the surest yield.

In order to grow seed, leave the plants in the ground over Winter and cover them lightly with leaves to protect them from the frost. The seed is harvested in the following season. Plants which bolt to seed the first season do not yield fertile seed.

PEAS

Varieties: 1. Smooth seeded sorts. These may early become hard and bitter, their only advantage being that because of greater hardiness they can be sown very early. For the home garden with limited space they may well be left out.

> Radio: 15 inches
> Alaska: 2½ feet.

2. Wrinkled seeded sorts. The pods of these varieties are large and full and the peas remain sweet for a longer time.

> Laxton's Progress: 18 inches.
> Little Marvel: 18 inches.
> Carter's Daisy: 2 feet.
> Alderman: 4½ to 6 feet.

3. Sugar peas. The green pods are eaten before the peas get large.

Usable varieties, Mammoth Melting Sugar: 5 feet, Dwarf White Sugar.

Sowing. The early smooth seeded varieties are sown in succession from March or April up to June.

Wrinkled varieties may not be sown before the middle of April. They are sensitive to frost in the seed. June sowings in warm localities often suffer from mildew.

Sow the dwarf varieties quite thickly, three rows per normal sized bed.

Of the taller varieties (which should have support) plant two rows in beds three feet or so wide. Two deep furrows are made with a pointed hoe about a foot from the center line of the bed on either side. Sow quite thinly, every inch or so a seed. After sowing, the furrows are covered with earth or compost and firmed with the back of a rake. Seed should be two to four inches deep. The peas can be protected from the birds by spreading fir branches or something similar over the beds until they have germinated.

Support. The branches of deciduous trees, pushed firmly in, down the center of the beds, offer the best and most natural support for pea vines. Chicken wire is more durable, of course. This is stretched down the center of the bed between strong end posts and braced at intervals with lighter stakes. A number of single wires can also be used. These are strung at six to eight inch intervals.

Support is given to the plants as soon as they tend to fall over and lie on the ground. At the same time, they should be hilled toward the center of the bed to guide the tendrils toward the supports.

Soil and fertilizer. A light, warm soil with some lime content is preferable for peas. Wrinkled peas also like heavier soils. The planting furrows receive preparation 500 and mild compost. Compost, from heaps which have had additions of horn or bone meal and wood ashes, is excellent. Preparation 501 is applied after the supports have been put up. Peas which are forced in any way always shoot into vine instead of setting pods. Keep clean of weeds!

Harvesting. Peas are carefully picked as they mature, taking care to preserve the tendrils of the plants. If possible, do not pick them in wet weather. (Danger of rust and mildew!) At the time of sowing it is necessary to estimate how many peas we can use, and to decide whether there will be enough time to pick them!

Seed stock. As peas cross with one another, it is good to separate the different varieties. The first and best pods should be left hanging for seed, and those which mature later picked for eating. A rigid policing is necessary because sparrows are very fond of peas. The seed pods should be healthy and uninjured. Hang them up under shelter to dry or better still let them ripen in the garden. Carrots and potatoes are good companion crops for peas.

STRING BEANS

1. Pole Beans.

Varieties: These are very numerous and there are many local variants. Kentucky Wonder and McCaslan are varieties which are good for home use and are marketable as well. The so-called Turkish or Fire bean is particularly hardy and suited to rough regions of high altitude.

Sowing. Pole beans are not sown before the middle of May and not later than June. In order to obtain a succession sow early and late maturing varieties at the same time. The hills should be three to three and a half feet apart. Set the poles singly with the help of a crowbar. It is not good to set a number together in the form of a wigwam. (Danger of mildew!) Plant eight or ten seeds around each pole not more than $1\frac{1}{2}$ inches deep. Either spray the planting holes with preparation 500 or add some compost earth before covering them. Watering is necessary in dry periods. However, cold water must not be used and the soil must be kept from crusting.

Soil and fertilizing. Pole beans require a fertile soil. Fertilize with good, prepared compost. If necessary, some applications of manure water may be given. Never use forcing fertilizers. Preparation 501 is applied just before they blossom.

Crop rotation. Pole beans may be planted everywhere. They are especially good for a soil which needs to be refreshed and built up again. Pole bean rows make a good wind-break.

Care. Break the soil up well by hoeing. Hill the plants toward the poles to guide the vines toward this support. They should be inspected occasionally to see that no tendrils have been torn down or have wandered away from the poles.

Harvesting. All of the beans ripe for picking should be carefully harvested. Otherwise, those left behind quickly get tough. Do not pull on the vines, but use a ladder!

Harmful pests and diseases. If possible, all garden beans as well as peas should not be touched as long as they are wet. The danger of fungus diseases is thus considerably lessened. As a preventive, spray weekly with equisetum tea, particularly during warm, moist weather or periods of sudden storms.

Should there be a sudden attack of black aphids they may be sprayed with a Quassia and soap solution. If it does not rain within two or three days, then this spray must be washed off thoroughly with water. In the meantime the lice will certainly have disappeared.

Seed selection. The first, best formed beans are left on the vine to ripen. Only May sowings guarantee the prospect of completely ripe seed stock.

Pole beans easily cross with each other, also with bush beans; this should be taken into consideration.

2. Bush Beans.

Varieties: These are also very numerous. Two excellent, heavy-bearing, stringless varieties are Tendergreen and Commodore. Stringless Black Valentine is especially good in drought.

Wax beans are more sensitive than green ones and easily become spotted, especially in wet weather. Pencil-Pod Black Wax and Brittle Wax are good varieties.

The beans used for baking, making soup, etc., are usually bush beans. Their cultivation is the same as for others, except that they are not harvested until ripe and are stored dry for Winter use. Certain varieties seem better suited to this purpose, such as Dwarf Horticultural, Red Kidney and White Marrowfat.

Sowing. Sowings at the end of April do not succeed every year. However, with favorable weather conditions, they yield the best-priced harvest. The first sure yields come from sowings made after the middle of May. Early varieties can be sown in succession up to the first of July. Sow four rows per bed, two seeds every four inches, or in hills, four or five seeds to a hill. The hills should be one and a half to two feet apart in all directions. Make the furrows four to five inches deep but cover the seed very lightly, about an inch and a half. "Beans should be able to hear the church bells ringing."

Cultural requirements. Bush beans like a warm soil and good compost fertilizing. They need water in dry periods but cannot stand either cold water or a crusted soil. It is better to water them thoroughly twice a week than to water superficially every day. Hoeing and two hillings are important to keep the soil fresh and to give them support.

Companion plants. Beans do well in alternation with beets, leeks, celeriac, and summer radishes, since they like to have a circulation of air. At the same time they have a good influence on their neighbors. They are a very good preparatory crop for every type of culture. Under certain circumstances, they do not mind following themselves.

Seed stock. The same rules apply to the harvest and selection of seed as with pole beans.

1. Pole Limas.

Varieties: King of the Garden is one of the many good varieties.

Sowing. This should be delayed, not only until danger of frost is past, but until the soil is thoroughly warm, as pole limas are the most tender of beans. Since they come into bearing somewhat later than the bush varieties, one sowing is enough for the season. Under normal conditions of moisture they will usually bear until frost kills the vines. Plant with the "eye" down. Poles about 7 feet high should be set at planting time, at least 3 feet apart in the row, with rows 4 feet apart. Vines can be pinched off at the tips when they reach the top of the pole.

Other details of sowing as well as of fertilizing, rotation, etc., are the same as for other pole beans.

2. Bush Limas.

Varieties: Fordhook Bush Lima is a good large-podded variety. There are also several kinds of Baby Limas which are delicious but more work to shell in quantity.

Sowing. Plant these also "eye" down, in rows. As they generally form more spreading plants than snap beans, they should be allowed a few extra inches in every direction. They are also more tender so that an early sowing is less certain to produce. Make succession sowings as for other bush beans. They mature more quickly than the pole limas and are slightly more hardy.

Further treatment is the same as for other bush beans.

BROAD BEANS

Varieties: The Windsor is the common type of Broad Bean, also sometimes called Fava Bean. It forms a stiff upright bush 2 to 4 feet high, very different in form from other beans. The

99

seed itself somewhat resembles a large lima but with the "eye" at the end.

Sowing. Hot and dry seasons do not suit broad beans, so they thrive best in Canada and the northern United States. Since they are much more hardy than other beans, they should be planted as early in the Spring as the ground can be worked so as to be well developed before Summer heat. Sow seed 6 inches apart, in rows 30 inches apart.

Cultural directions. Those given for other beans may be followed.

Harvesting. They are sometimes eaten with the pod, but for this must be picked when very young. At a somewhat later stage they may be shelled and cooked like fresh lima beans. If allowed to ripen, they can be kept dry for Winter use. In this case the tough outer skin of the bean will need to be removed after cooking. They have a flavor quite different from other beans and are especially rich in protein.

EARLY POTATOES

Varieties: Irish Cobbler and Early Rose.

Planting time: April.

Pregermination. The potatoes are spread out on trestles in a light room to form firm, green sprouts. The maximum temperature of the room should be around 55 degrees Fahrenheit. Pregermination gives an earlier harvest. However, presprouted potatoes are more sensitive to frost. The rows should be two feet apart, distance apart in the row, one and a half to two feet.

Soil and fertilizer. Early potatoes belong in the "first rank." They are planted in ground which has had prepared manure spaded or ploughed under in the Fall and has been left over Winter in rough clods. Preparation 500 is sprayed before planting. According to the usage of the locality early potatoes are planted with a spade or a mattock.

Summer care. Potatoes should be hoed as soon as possible. When the plants have grown taller hoe them again and hill them. They should be hilled for a second time before the plants have covered the patch so thickly that it is impossible to get between them.

Shortly after the first and second hilling spray with preparation 501. Repeated sprayings of equisetum tea are necessary, especially during warm, humid weather.

Harvesting. Potatoes are dug as soon as the vines have wilted. Prepare the ground immediately with a spade or mattock for the succeeding crop. Brussels sprouts, kale, spinach, endive and others may follow early potatoes.

Seed stock. For a seed stock choose *only* perfectly healthy, scab-free potatoes from healthy plants surrounded by plants which are also healthy. The plants should be marked beforehand, and the potatoes dug before harvesting the others. Store these very carefully, over Winter, dry and frost free, in the cellar or in a pit. They require good ventilation. The best way to store them is to bury them in layers of dry sand and spray them with preparation 501. Potatoes stored in this way keep very well.

TOMATOES

Varieties: Pritchard and Marglobe, Bonny Best, John Baer, Penn State Earliana.

The fruits should be full-fleshed, round and smooth, not ridged and not too seedy. The skin should be firm and not easily split. There are, of course, many more varieties than the two mentioned. Almost every year the seed houses present new ones.

Sowing. Tomatoes are sown in flats or hotbeds about the middle of March.

Transplanting. They should be transplanted after the unfolding of the second leaves into flats or coldframes to stand about three or four inches apart. It is excellent practice to transplant them for a second time. At this time they may be put in four-inch pots, if desired. At every transplanting they should be set deeper.

Setting out. Tomatoes are set out from the 20th to the 25th of May. They should be set out just before blossoming. Plant them in rows three feet or more apart, according to the type of cultivation, two to two and a half feet apart in the rows. The planting hills are dug out and filled with compost. The plants, with good, undisturbed root balls, are set in the holes a bit on a slant in order to bring as much stem under the ground as possible. Spray preparation 500 in the plant holes as well as on the rest of the ground. Tread the earth down firmly around the roots of the plants and water. Six foot poles are then set firmly on the weather side of the .plants.

Fertilizing. Rich prepared mixed compost or prepared manure, not yet completely rotted, mixed with compost made from the tomato's own refuse, suits these peculiar plants best. Besides, they are not included in the crop rotation. Contrary to the behaviour of all other annual, cultivated plants, they develop best when they are planted in the same place every year. Abundant fertilizing is therefore necessary every year. This peculiarity of tomatoes makes it convenient to grow them on a trellis always against the same wall or otherwise under some slight glass protection. The last is good since they cannot stand sudden pouring rain and storms.

Summer care. Preparation 501 is applied after the plants are well established. (Repeat in two weeks time.) Hill them very high. Tomatoes are grateful, if the ground is watered, but they cannot stand being sprayed with a hose or even the watering can. Use water that has stood open to the sun and air. Mulching, with straw compost, for example, is a very good practice.

Pruning. Too rank a growth of foliage delays the ripening of the fruit. Leave one or two main stems and cut the side shoots out of the axils. Large leaves should never be removed. The main stalk may be topped, if necessary. This is done when growth is too strong at the cost of the ripening of the fruit. However, it should never be done before September.

Weekly sprayings of equisetum tea (which sticks better when a small amount of clay is added) as well as of preparation 501 are beneficial to the health of tomatoes.

Inter-cropping. In view of the many operations necessary for the care of tomatoes inter-cropping is not expedient. With a distance of three feet between the rows a row of New Zealand spinach can be alternated with a row of tomatoes. (Every six feet a tomato row.)

Seed growing. Choose healthy, early-ripening, well-formed fruits from good plants. These should not be left on the stalks until they are over-ripe, but should be picked before this. Later, when they have become dark red, scrape out the seeds. Set these in a little water and allow them to ferment. Then put them in a sieve and wash them off well under the faucet. Spread out on blotting paper to dry.

The process of ripening and fermentation must not be too long drawn out. It can happen that the seeds begin to germinate in the flesh of the fruit.

Storing. When the first night frosts seem imminent, dig the plants up, hang them up by the roots in a warm place (kitchen) and, in this way, let the green tomatoes ripen.

We have had good, tasty tomatoes until Christmas, when we stored them in this way.

RHUBARB

Varieties: Myatt's Victoria and MacDonald are good red-stalked types.

Planting. Rhubarb is a perennial plant, which cannot, therefore, be included in the crop rotation. In the first year bush beans, peas, early savoy cabbage, kohl-rabi, lettuce, or spinach may be grown between the rows.

Roots are set out in October or in March, four to six feet apart in all directions. (In a small garden it can be planted on the edge or in the lowest lying, moistest corner.) Rhubarb can stand light shade. It is sensitive to poor soil drainage.

Soil and fertilizer requirements. Rhubarb will reward us with abundant yields for many years, if we plant it in a good, fresh, deep soil where it can have lots of moisture and nutritive substance. Deep cultivation of the soil is necessary in preparation for a rhubarb planting. Instead of simply turning the ground with a spade it should be trenched. A trench is dug which is a spade wide and a spade deep. The first or upper spades full of earth are put aside. The earth on the bottom of the trench is then broken up and turned over. Then it is filled up with the upper soil layers of the next trench. Again, the bottom of the second trench is turned with the spade and so on, until finally the earth, which was put aside, serves to fill the last trench. The end result is a one and a half spade deep cultivation of the ground, and the topsoil is still above, and the subsoil remains underneath. Manure can, of course, be put in the upper layer, where it will work effectively because the soil is aerated. Such deep trenching must be done in the Autumn.

A heavy application of well-composted, prepared manure is given at the time of planting. Afterward, the plants are mulched with strawy manure compost or leaf compost.

In later years, the rhubarb patch is no longer spaded, but manure is criled in, in the Fall, and preparation 500 sprayed. When it begins to sprout in the Spring it should receive some compost. It should be watered with manure water after every heavy picking. This is very essential after the last picking of the season. Spray preparation 501 before the first picking and two weeks after the last.

Harvesting. We can begin to pick rhubarb after the third year. Never take more than one third of the stalks at one time. The stalks are not cut, but are pulled with caution (with a slight

104

twisting movement) so as to spare the main buds. Blossom stems must be pulled out at the base. However, this should not be done when heavy pickings are being made. Otherwise, the plants could be weakened.

Seed culture does not come into consideration for the gardener since seedlings often do not run true to type.

Strawberries find their place in the small garden, usually in alternation with beds of vegetables. So room may be made for them also in the chapter on vegetable culture, in this little book.

Varieties:
> Early: Premier (Howard 17), Dorsett, Dunlap.
> Mid-season: Catskill.
> Late: Chesapeake, Gaudy Redheart.

Cultural requirements. The shallow rooting, heavy bearing strawberry plants need a certain amount of air and soil moisture, but also light and warmth in order to set blossoms and fruit. A light, sandy soil with a good humus content, a soil which has been cultivated for years and is protected against drying out, is the most suitable for them. In heavy, cold soils, they never develop the fine fragrance which they have when they are grown in true strawberry soil. Through the skillful use of the bio-dynamic sprays and prepared composts, we can, however, create a certain "strawberry climate" and favorable soil conditions even in unsuitable localities.

Planting. August and September plantings often succeed better than those made in the Spring. The soil is prepared as usual. It should not, however, be cultivated too deeply. The land chosen should be as free of weeds as possible. The trenching method described in rhubarb culture may be used under certain circumstances. The furrows or plant holes are sprayed with preparation 500 and then partly filled with some good, well-ripened compost.

Wide spacing is best for strawberries, two rows on a three foot bed, eight to ten inches apart in the row. Raised beds are used in very wet locations or heavy soils. Rows of bush beans can be planted between the strawberry rows the first year. Later, the strawberries will have so covered the beds that inter-cropping is impossible.

Care and fertilizing. After planting, mulch the beds with good, ripe manure, taking care not to cover the plants, which rot easily. This manure is left on the surface for a winter mulch. In the Spring spray preparation 500. Cultivate lightly with a crile or rake between the rows. If the winter mulch has rotted and disappeared into the soil, somewhat, add a new light mulch. Spruce or pine needles have proven to be by far the best for this purpose. New, raw needles must not be used, however. These should first be composted with layers of half-ripe compost, prepared, and let stand to decompose. Such a clean mulch eliminates the necessity of spreading shavings under the ripening fruit—always an unsatisfactory practice. Scrupulous weeding is necessary and rewarding. Mulching makes weeding easier.

Preparation 501 is sprayed as soon as the plants have formed green and whitish berries. Equisetum tea is sprayed before blossoming as a preventive against fungous diseases. This is repeated as often as is necessary. Do not, however, spray during blossoming or during ripening.

Increase. Right after the plants have stopped bearing, remove the runners, clean the beds, and select the oldest and strongest runners for increase. Only young plants taken from one year old beds should be used. It is often customary to set out new beds every year to make sure of always having new young plants. However, strawberry beds which have been cared for as we have described above, often continue to bear well for as long as five or six years. When this is the case, it pays of course to let them stand.

It is best not to leave the runner plants attached to the mother plant. They should be removed and set out in a coldframe or a

106

sheltered garden bed. (Portable coldframes are useful for this.) A sandy soil, spraying with preparation 500, careful maintenance of moisture and protection from the full sun, all help them to root quickly.

After removing the runners the cleaned bed should be hoed or criled. The mulch is worked into the soil somewhat from this cultivation so it should be renewed again. At the end of the season remove all the newly developed runners and all old, spotted leaves. The bed is then hoed or criled again and a winter mulch of well-rotted manure compost is applied.

There are everbearing types of strawberries which are grown from seed. These are often used in the small garden as border plantings. Runnerless varieties are particularly suited to this, Rugen, or Baron Solemacher, for example. A good everbearing variety, which makes runners, is Mastodon. (See Pennsylvania State Circular 181, page 10.)

REGARDING THE USE OF THE PREPARATIONS

We have already gone into the application of the bio-dynamic preparations under all the different cultures and have given special instructions for the spray preparations 500 and 501. Each time we have indicated the correct point in the development of the different plants at which these sprays should be applied. In the home garden, with mixed cultures and intercropping the gardener will not be able to apply them correctly to every individual culture. He will, then, limit himself to spraying preparation 500 on the open soil at the chief planting times. This must, of course, be lightly criled or raked into the soil. He will use preparation 501 so that the main crops are benefited. As far as possible, he will avoid blossoming or harvest ripe plants when spraying 501. This preparation will be used from one to three times during the Summer on those plants which need it most, that is, the plants which should develop a healthy leaf growth.

The *general* effect of the spray preparations has been described in Chapter III.

There are, however, still some details concerning the use of equisetum tea which have not yet been mentioned. (Preparation 508.) This tea (Equisetum arvense) was recommended by Dr. Rudolf Steiner as a spray against all kinds of fungus diseases in horticulture and agriculture. If consistently applied, this simple remedy has always proven itself in practice. The tea is prepared in the following manner. It is started in cold water, boiled for not longer than twenty minutes and is then allowed to cool gradually. Use one portion of equisetum (¾ oz.) to 1 quart (4 cups) of water. After cooking, this tea is diluted in 1 gallon of water preparatory to spraying. Stir the solution thoroughly for 10 minutes, using the same technique as for 500. In early Spring spray it as a preventive measure. During warm, wet weather and acute fungus attacks apply the tea repeatedly as long as it seems necessary. Further instructions have been given under the individual cultures.

7. Herbs in the Farm and Home Garden

THE USE of herbs for purposes of healing and as ingredients in food is indeed as old as humanity itself. A general fund of knowledge concerning them has grown up out of experience in the course of millennia. Men who knew the secrets of herbs and their effects were especially venerated in the past. The use of herbs was first discredited by the quackery and other mischief which was ascribed in the Middle Ages to the so-called "herb-women." However, even in the present day, aromatic plants are still used as pot herbs, particularly in France and all southern countries. Otherwise they have been displaced more and more by the products of the steadily developing chemical industry. Many of the chemicals present in herbs have been produced in a pure form or they have even been produced synthetically. Indeed, the further development of this chemical science now shows that the so-called pure substance does not always exhibit the highest degree of aroma, a fact which has been most clearly illustrated in the manufacture of perfumes. The highest degree of aroma and the greatest medicinal effect come to expression just in that mixture which nature creates through the co-operation of the earth with the sun and its radiant energies. Up to the present, chemical science has not been able to imitate this particular combination of forces.

Recently, the tendency to turn back to the use of unadulterated natural substances has become increasingly apparent. Although to a large extent, the chemist still rules supreme in the production of medicaments, the chemical factory has not yet been able to completely conquer the realm of the kitchen. For a good housewife and cook knows how very far the substitutes lag behind the natural substances in quality and fragrance.

A house without the fresh faces of children, without their merry, frequently unexpected pranks, often seems a tiresome place to us. So a garden without flowers and herbs, without glowing colors and fragrance, is also boring. Boredom is not only disagreeable, but those who are not able to shake it off can even be made ill by it. In the same way, dishes, in which no spicy herbs are found, are not only insipid, but they may even disagree with one. The cultivation of spices and aromatic herbs in the small garden is therefore well justified. It cannot be termed luxury to make room in it for all kinds of flowers and herbs as well as for the necessary vegetables.

We have already described the role which aromatic plants and blossoming herbs play in the vegetable garden, in Chapter IV. More exact information about the cultivation of medicinal herbs may be obtained from Department of Agriculture Bulletins. Details concerning the application of the bio-dynamic method to their cultivation may be found in an article by Franz Lippert, *Zur Praxis des Heilpflanzenanbaues,* (The Practical Cultivation of Medicinal Plants.)

There are certain general cultural requirements for herbs which may be mentioned. Just those plants which should develop a fine aroma do not achieve this when they are heavily and freshly manured, frequently watered or forced with liquid manure. A strong, rank growth of the leaf and stem on the one side and the development of aroma on the other represent a kind of antithesis in the plant. In the case of herbs, there is a loss of etheric oils corresponding to rank growth, therefore a loss of that which gives aromatic plants their value.

Essentially, herbs need a warm, weed-free, not meagre, but also not an over-rich soil and in most cases a sunny location. They like a circulation of air and the possibility of spreading out. The decorative amongst them, such as parsley, savory, thyme, chives and sometimes marjoram lend themselves to use as borders for the garden beds. Some of the most cherished aromatic herbs, such as rosemary and annual basil, need a great deal of warmth. It would be better to make room for these on the window sill than to set them out in the garden.

We will go on now to individual descriptions of some of the most important annual and perennial herbs and details of their culture.

GARDEN CRESS

Garden cress, also called Curled or Peppergrass Cress, is a familiar sight to all the children of Europe for it is often grown indoors on a plate of moist cotton. It grows there in the warm kitchen just as well as it does later in the garden. It yields the first, fresh, spring salad. Garden cress should be sown fairly thickly, but only a very little at one time, in pots and flats, in the corner of a cold-frame or in light compost on the edge of a garden bed. The seeds need not necessarily be covered with earth. Water and shade it when necessary. It grows very quickly and is ready to be cut in about a week. More than two cuttings are impracticable. It is better to pull the old cress out and make repeated sowings every two weeks until hot weather sets in and cress becomes peppery.

It is very difficult to gather seed from it because the seeds fall out readily and are liked very much by the birds. Already in the second year cress seed germinates very poorly.

DILL

Dill is sown in March/April right where we wish it to grow. Do not sow it too thickly, and cover it lightly with earth. If necessary, the sowing is thinned. Since no great amount of it is needed for use, light inter-sowings are often made in carrot, lettuce, onion, or cucumber beds.

If we want dill to form good seeds we must not let the plants stand too close together. Dill seeds ripen easily and also drop out very readily. It grows very easily and is quite apt to become a weed. We need not fear that it will disappear from the garden.

Dill is used principally as a salad herb. It helps to make cucumber salad more digestible. It is also a good seasoning for fish dishes and potatoes.

BORAGE

The characteristic black seeds of borage sometimes germinate with difficulty, sometimes easily. When it is necessary to transplant them, this should be done while they are young and with great care, as they do not like being moved. If we have once had the rough-leaved, beautiful, blue-blossomed plant in the garden, however, it remains faithful for years. The young leaves have a fresh cucumber flavor. They are used especially as a seasoning for head lettuce salad and cottage cheese. Borage is also excellent bee pasture.

SWEET MARJORAM

In its Mediterranean home, marjoram is a perennial, and here it can be brought indoors for Winter protection and kept over from year to year, making an unusually attractive house plant. It is best to sow the very fine seed in a flat in a warm, light room. The tiny plants are later pricked out in little bunches of two to four, for which task tweezers must be used. They are transplanted a second time into a frame and are set out in the open after the middle of May. The small gardener generally prefers to purchase seedlings and set them out at the proper time in a sunny bed border.

Cutting can begin as soon as the round buds of the blossoms have formed in the leaf axils.

Marjoram is used in egg dishes, in sausage and all kinds of meat dishes. It makes these more stimulating in flavor and therefore more digestible. It acts as a kind of preservative and is also important in veterinary medicine.

ANNUAL OR SUMMER SAVORY

Savory is just as fine-seeded as marjoram. However, it can be sown in the open in March/April. Later the seedlings should be transplanted to stand about six inches apart. It demands little in respect of soil but likes sunshine. Perennial or Winter savory has a more biting flavor than the annual type. Both readily find their place as the edging of a garden bed.

The shoots are cut at the same time as those of marjoram and thyme, before blossoming. It is especially good for seasoning peas, beans, and tomatoes.

PARSLEY

Everyone is familiar with the curled type of parsley, Extra Curled Dwarf, for example. Few people know, however, that smooth-leaved parsley is far more aromatic than the curly leaved. Smooth parsley is rarely planted because people are afraid of confusing it with Poison Hemlock (Conium maculatum) or with Dog's Parsley (Aethusa cynapium). However, the fragrance of true parsley is unmistakable.

The use of parsley root as a soup flavor (like celery) is very little known in America. It might be a good idea to experiment with root parsley. (Parsnip-Rooted or Hamburg Parsley.)

Parsley is one of the most widely used and indispensable herbs. It stimulates the kidneys, that is, it speeds up the removal of waste matter from the body. It also helps in the digestion of heavy, slowly digested foods. Does not this remind us of potato salad?

Root parsley is sown as soon as the ground is open. It is good to mark the rows with radish seed. Cultivation and treatment are the same as for carrots. The plants pulled out when thinning can be used for soup greens. Parsley for cutting (smooth or curled) is sown broadcast in fine compost on the edge of a garden bed or in some corner or other. The seed should be well firmed and watered.

All parsley winters over well. It yields its main crop in the Spring of the second year. It is very simple to harvest seed from strong plants which are left standing about a foot apart. Cut the stems as soon as the main umbels have turned dark brown. These are dried in an airy place under shelter. When they are quite dry the seeds are rubbed out by hand. Our own experience has been that home-grown seed stock has a high percentage of germination, though all parsley seed is slow to germinate.

CHIVES

In the Fall or early Spring plant bulbs taken from old plants, in a fresh, somewhat moist, loamy soil. Chives can be harvested all Summer if, instead of cutting lawn-mower fashion, each leaf is cut individually and not too many at one time from any one plant. It makes an ornamental as well as a useful border.

THYME

The summer warmth requirements of thyme are similar to those of marjoram. However thyme is more hardy and winters over, with light protection, until it falls a victim to a particularly severe Winter. It likes a dry, sunny location and a sandy soil. Sow in the open in March/April. Re-set the plants in the Fall, ten to twelve inches apart. It is preferable to buy seedlings for the home or kitchen garden, as in the case of marjoram.

Thyme is harvested in the same way as savory and marjoram. Its uses are similar to those of marjoram but it is perhaps more many-sided. It can, for instance, be added to the bath; then it has a strengthening effect.

SAGE

Sage is an old and renowned medicinal herb. It is still used as a remedy for colds. In America, however, it is most frequently used as a seasoning in turkey and chicken dressing.

Sage plants are set out in the Fall in well cultivated land. Put good compost in the plant holes. One or two plants are enough to give the small gardener an abundance of this herb.

HYSSOP

Hyssop is planted and cared for in the same way as sage. It needs light winter protection, however. Otherwise it is very undemanding. It should be gathered before blossoming. Its fine, pungent leaves are used like savory. The rather small, deep-blue blossom panicles are decorative and very attractive to the bees.

LEMON BALM (MELISSA OFFICINALIS)

Lemon balm is beloved as a salad herb, an ingredient of sauces and as a tea. The plants are increased by division, in the Fall or Spring. Should they get too large and sprawly divide them and set them out anew. In Switzerland, where this plant is native, it is apt to get too wild if not held somewhat in check. However, it scarcely can be termed a weed even then.

TARRAGON

Tarragon is valued as a salad herb and as an ingredient of cucumber pickles, also for making a fine vinegar. The true French Tarragon seldom blooms and never sets fertile seed here, so it must be propagated from cuttings or root division. Seed offered for sale is probably from a Siberian variety, inferior in flavor though somewhat hardier in growth. Tarragon is different from many herbs in tolerating some shade and moisture, but it *must* have a well-drained situation. In the small garden we must take care to cut it at the proper time; blossoming plants lose their fragrance. In time, the plants get very large and must often be divided. This should be taken into consideration when setting them out.

SWEET BASIL

Sweet Basil, or Herbe Royale as it is called in France, is one of a large family of basils, most of them natives of India. Hence it is one of the most tender plants of the herb garden, and the seeds, sown anew each Spring, should not be exposed to frosts. It transplants well and likes full sun. It will grow into a bushy plant about 18 inches high, so allow plenty of space for it. The leaves are used for flavoring soups and stews, tomato dishes, and a few finely chopped add piquancy to a lettuce salad. We may start to pick them while the plant is still small, but the harvest for drying should take place just as the inconspicuous buds are ready to open. Even after severe cutting the plants usually grow out again, and a plant or two can be brought into the house before frost to provide fresh leaves all Winter.

ROSEMARY

The Herb of Remembrance is best known of all in history and legend. Its fragrant, dark, gray-green, narrow leaves look much like needles. They are evergreen too, but in most climates the plant must be brought indoors to survive the Winter, since its native home is on the shores of the Mediterranean. There on the rocky slopes overlooking the sea, it grows to be a large shrub; but in our gardens after several years it may not be over 2 or 3 feet tall. Still it is a charming, sturdy plant with woody branches that often take peculiar turns and twists. The pale blue flowers are small and do not appear for a year or two. A sunny, well-drained location suits it. Propagation is easy, either from cuttings or seeds. The latter are slow to germinate. Occasionally it is used in meat dishes, but its fragrance alone is enough to justify the presence of one plant even in the smallest garden.

LOVAGE

Lovage is a mighty, out-spreading plant, which often reaches a height of six or eight feet. We must, therefore, allow quite a bit of room in the garden for it. A heavy soil and a somewhat moist location please it. The plants last for years and are very thankful for a winter mulch of good ripe manure. Lovage is a spicy herb which was well-known in ancient times. In the kitchen it is used in all kinds of soups, sauces, meat and vegetable dishes. The root is also used in medicine.

We shall close our consideration of herbs with lovage, one of the largest of their representatives. They are all friendly helpers of man and contribute to his health. As such, they should be still more valued in many places, than is true today.

8. A Manifesto to the Housewife

WE HAVE briefly described everything necessary for the production of vegetables in the small garden. If our instructions are accurately and diligently followed, and the weather is willing, we are certain that one day you will have the finest vegetables for your table.

The best, most nourishing, tastiest vegetables, however, can be completely ruined if they are cooked to death. We beg you, therefore, to treat the fruits of your labor with consideration. Vegetables should be prepared so that all the original nutritive substances and flavors are preserved and not exhausted or evaporated through hour-long cooking (and then warming over).

Fine vegetables keep well and have a piquant flavor. The water in which they are cooked has a pleasant taste and can very well be used as soup stock or to make vegetable bouillon. If the cooking water has a bitter, salty, soapy, or flat taste, then the fertilizer is surely at fault. Like fertilizer, like flavor.

There is satisfaction for the home gardener when he or she succeeds in producing good vegetables of fine flavor. However, complete satisfaction only comes when these are prepared so that they are still fresh and stimulating in flavor, and not just like "any other old vegetable from the market."

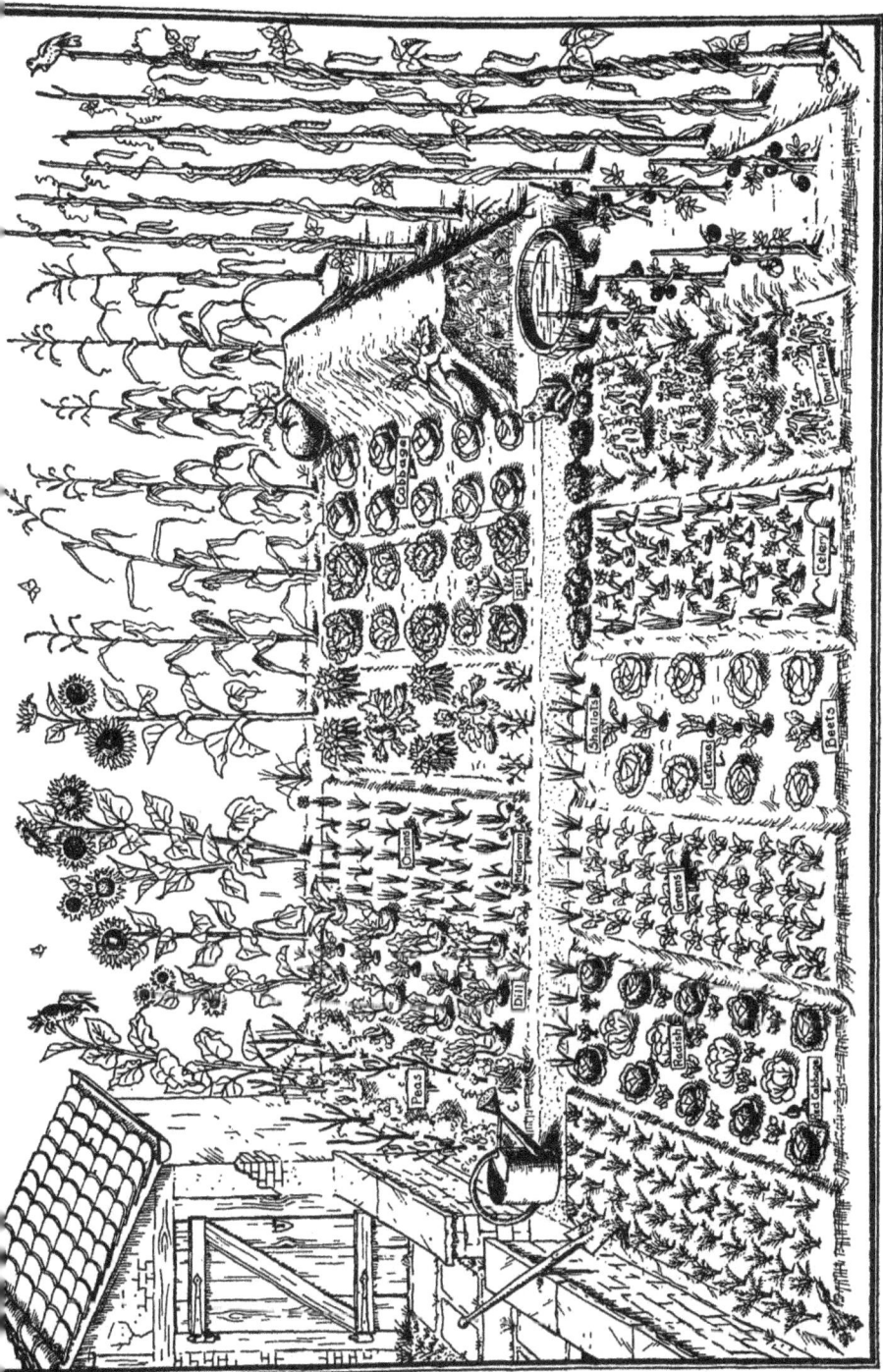

www.ingramcontent.com/pod-product-compliance
Lightning Source LLC
Chambersburg PA
CBHW022012090426
42741CB00007B/1003